A WORKBOOK FOR SELF-STUDY

READING & WRITING KOREAN

A Beginner's Guide to the Hangeul Writing System

Jieun Kiaer and Derek Driggs

Mnemonic Illustrations by Jessica Anecito

TUTTLE Publishing

Tokyo | Rutland, Vermont | Singapore

"Books to Span the East and West"

Tuttle Publishing was founded in 1832 in the small New England town of Rutland, Vermont [USA]. Our core values remain as strong today as they were then—to publish best-in-class books which bring people together one page at a time. In 1948, we established a publishing outpost in Japan—and Tuttle is now a leader in publishing English-language books about the arts, languages and cultures of Asia. The world has become a much smaller place today and Asia's economic and cultural influence has grown. Yet the need for meaningful dialogue and information about this diverse region has never been greater. Over the past seven decades, Tuttle has published thousands of books on subjects ranging from martial arts and paper crafts to language learning and literature—and our talented authors, illustrators, designers and photographers have won many prestigious awards. We welcome you to explore the wealth of information available on Asia at **www.tuttlepublishing.com**.

Published by Tuttle Publishing, an imprint of Periplus Editions (HK) Ltd.

www.tuttlepublishing.com

Copyright © 2021 by Periplus Editions (HK) Ltd.

All rights reserved.

Library of Congress Catalog-in-Publication Data in progress

ISBN 978-0-8048-5308-8

First edition, 2021

Photo and illustration credits: page 73 sasimo-to; page 76 kaisom; page 77 LMspencer; page 80 Cherstva; page 86 Silvia Elizabeth Pangaro; page 94 GoodStudio. All Shutterstock.com.

Distributed by

North America, Latin America & Europe
Tuttle Publishing
364 Innovation Drive
North Clarendon,
VT 05759-9436 U.S.A.
Tel: 1 (802) 773-8930; Fax: 1 (802) 773-6993
info@tuttlepublishing.com
www.tuttlepublishing.com

Asia Pacific
Berkeley Books Pte. Ltd.
3 Kallang Sector #04-01
Singapore 349278
Tel: (65) 6741-2178; Fax: (65) 6741-2179
inquiries@periplus.com.sg
www.tuttlepublishing.com

26 25 24 23   5 4 3
Printed in Malaysia   2301VP

TUTTLE PUBLISHING® is a registered trademark of Tuttle Publishing, a division of Periplus Editions (HK) Ltd.

Contents

How to Use This Book

Who is this book for?
This book is designed for learners of Korean who wish to learn to read and write using the Hangeul alphabet. It is aimed at beginning-level students, and no prior knowledge of Korean is required. It can be used by self-study students or in a classroom.

What is the purpose of this book?
The purpose of this book is to introduce the letters of the Hangeul alphabet and to provide plentiful practice material so that students can learn the basics of reading and writing. The practice exercises in the book use words and phrases that are common in contemporary Korea, covering useful topics such as numbers, food, K-pop and social media.

How is the book structured?
This book is divided into two main parts. **Part One** starts by introducing the six basic vowels and nine basic consonants of the Hangeul alphabet, and shows how they combine to make syllables. Memorable illustrations help students learn and remember the sound and shape of each letter. Part One then introduces aspirated consonants, double consonants and diphthongs.

Each section of Part One has handwriting practice boxes showing the stroke order of each letter, along with reading practice exercises so that students can identify the new letters learned in everyday vocabulary words, and regular review exercises. By the end of Part One, students will have practiced reading and writing all the letters and syllables of the Hangeul alphabet.

Part Two presents everyday Korean vocabulary grouped into various subject categories, with handwriting exercises as well as challenging and fun reading and writing activities. A key at the back of the book provides answers to all the exercises.

Online audio recordings are provided to accompany the sections of the book marked with a headphones logo, to help students learn the pronunciation of letters, syllables and words. Free downloadable flash cards help students learn the letters and vocabulary quickly. Audio recordings and downloadable flash cards can be accessed using the link on page 6.

An Overview of the Korean Writing System

Korean uses an alphabet which is phonetic like the English alphabet. It is composed of vowels and consonants, which are combined into syllables to spell out words. There are twenty-one vowels in Korean and nineteen consonants. While English syllables are formed by aligning letters horizontally from left to right, Korean letters are arranged in boxes made up of consonants (C) and vowels (V), in the following possible configurations:

CV	C	CV	CV	C	C
	V	C	CC	V	V
				C	CC

These syllables are read out from left to right and from top to bottom. The above configurations are introduced gradually as you work your way through this book.

A Brief History of Hangeul

From speech to writing

There are about 6,000 languages in the world but only 250 different writing systems, 40 of which are actively in use. Of the 40, Hangeul is the only alphabet in the world for which the maker, the creation process, and the reason for its creation are fully known. It is the only deliberately created writing system in wide use today, invented approximately 600 years ago by King Sejong (1397–1450), although it was only in 1894 that the Korean alphabet, or Hangeul, came to be used as the official writing system for the Korean language.

Before Hangeul

Before Hangeul was invented, Koreans used two languages. Their spoken language was Korean, but their written language was classical Chinese, as this was the only script available to them. At first, Koreans adopted only the Chinese characters which referred to proper nouns—such as the names of people, villages, rivers, mountains, and so on. Later, they began to write whole sentences in Chinese. The use of Chinese for writing was far from ideal, because Chinese and Korean are very different languages. In Chinese, word order is rigid and the verb is placed directly after the subject, as in English. But in Korean, word order is flexible and the verb normally comes at the end of a sentence. The sound systems of both languages are also very different. Ordinary people with no formal education therefore had no way to express themselves in writing. This is the reason why King Sejong invented the Hangeul alphabet.

King Sejong the Great: the creator of Hangeul

King Sejong the Great was not only a leader, he was also a brilliant scholar. Most historians believe that he created Hangeul by himself. In 1443 King Sejong announced the invention of a new alphabet designed to improve literacy among the ordinary people. In the *Hunminjeongum Haerye*, the manuscript he wrote to promulgate the new alphabet, he says:

> *The speech sounds of Korea are distinct from those of China and thus are not communicable with Chinese characters. Hence, many people having something to put into words are unable to express their feelings. To overcome such distressing circumstances, I have newly devised twenty-eight letters that everyone can learn with ease and use with convenience in daily life.*

However, although King Sejong and his successors took great pains to encourage the use of Hangeul, it took almost 500 years before the alphabet became the official writing system.

The use of Hangeul: for and against

Hangeul was not embraced immediately by all. Many high-profile members of government and nobles thought that using Chinese characters symbolized Korea's advanced civilization and connection to China's power, and that it also distinguished Koreans from other people who were considered barbarians. As a result, the Korean alphabet was not used in official documents, although it flourished among the common people, who finally had a way to write down their own language, exactly as King Sejong had hoped.

In the early twentieth century, when Korea was struggling against colonization by Japan, Hangeul came to be seen as a patriotic symbol of this struggle. During this time, Hangeul was standardized and began to be used in newspapers and other publications. Soon it became the main writing system in Korea, for both common and official purposes.

Today, all official documents are written in Hangeul and it is used by all Koreans, in the North and the South. King Sejong's vision of a universal Korean writing system has been realized.

Korean romanization systems

As Korea became globalized, it became necessary to create a system of romanization for use by non-Korean speakers. Several romanization systems were developed, including the main ones shown below, all of which are quite different. All three romanized words below are the same Korean word, 음절, which means *syllable*:

Yale romanization:	**umcel**
McCune Reischauer romanization:	**ŭmchŏl**
Revised romanization:	**eumjeol**

For native English speakers, none of these systems is really intuitive. The Korean language has many sounds with no exact equivalent in English, so romanized spellings of words can be difficult to read and pronounce. The Revised Romanization System was developed and released by the Korean government in the year 2000, and is now the commonly used system for official communications in South Korea. This is the romanization system we use in this book.

You can practice the correct pronunciation of each Korean syllable and word by listening to the accompanying audio recordings available on the Tuttle website at the link below:

To access the online audio recordings and printable flashcards for this book

1. Check that you have an Internet connection.
2. Type the following URL into your web browser.
   www.tuttlepublishing.com/reading-and-writing-korean

For support, you can email us at info@tuttlepublishing.com.

PART ONE

Reading and Writing Hangeul: The Basics

This section introduces the basic vowels and consonants of Hangeul and shows you how to combine them to make syllables. Each syllable is introduced with handwriting practice boxes showing the stroke order followed by reading practice exercises so that you can identify the syllables learned in everyday vocabulary words. Regular review exercises are included. By the end of Part One, you will have practiced writing and reading all the letters and syllables of the Hangeul alphabet!

BASIC KOREAN VOWELS AND CONSONANTS

Korean has six basic vowels and nine basic consonants. The six basic vowels can be combined with each other and with six "y" vowels to make a total of twenty-one vowel sounds (see Complex Vowels on page 52). The nine basic consonants can be doubled or aspirated (pronounced with an extra breath of air) to make a total of nineteen consonants (see Aspirated Consonants on page 30 and Doubled Consonants on page 42).

Korean vowels and consonants are never written separately. They are always written in combination to form syllables. The vowels ㅏ a, ㅓ eo and ㅣ i are always attached to the right of the consonant. The vowels ㅗ o, ㅜ u and ㅡ eu are always attached to the bottom of the consonant. This section will help you memorize the basic vowels and consonants before learning how to write them in combination from page 12 onwards.

🎧 The Six Basic Vowels

Listen to the online audio recordings for each vowel, and then write the vowel using the grid lines to guide you.

ㅏ
a

The vowel ㅏ is pronounced **ah** as in father.

✍ **Practice writing ㅏ**

f<u>a</u>ther

ㅓ
eo

The vowel ㅓ is pronounced **uh** as in mother, but it is pronounced with the lips rounded.

✍ **Practice writing ㅓ**

m<u>o</u>ther

ㅣ
i

The vowel ㅣ is pronounced **ee** as in tree.

✍ **Practice writing ㅣ**

tr<u>ee</u>

⊥
o

The vowel ⊥ is pronounced **oh** as in boat.

✎ **Practice writing** ⊥

boat

T
u

The vowel T is pronounced **oo** as in root.

✎ **Practice writing** T

root

—
eu

The vowel — is pronounced **uh** as in foot.

✎ **Practice writing** —

foot

🎧 The Nine Basic Consonants

Listen to the online pronunciations for each consonant, and then write the consonant using the grid lines to guide you.

ㄱ
g

The consonant ㄱ has a **g** sound, similar to the one in gun, but slightly softer, somewhere between a **g** and a **k**.

✎ **Practice writing** ㄱ

gun

ㄴ
n

The consonant ㄴ makes an **n** sound, as in nap.

✍ **Practice writing ㄴ**

ㄴ	ㄴ								

nap

ㄷ
d

The consonant ㄷ makes a **d** sound, as in dinosaur.

✍ **Practice writing ㄷ**

ㄷ	ㄷ								

dinosaur

ㄹ
r / l

The consonant ㄹ does not have an equivalent sound in English, but is somewhere between **r** as in rattlesnake and **l** as in lake.

✍ **Practice writing ㄹ**

ㄹ	ㄹ								

rattlesnake

ㅁ
m

The consonant ㅁ makes an **m** sound, as in mug.

✍ **Practice writing ㅁ**

ㅁ	ㅁ								

mug

ㅂ
b

The consonant **ㅂ** makes a soft **b** sound, as in *b*oy, but with a little more air in the **b** sound.

✍ Practice writing ㅂ

bucket

ㅅ
s

The consonant **ㅅ** makes an **s** sound, as in *s*tanding.

✍ Practice writing ㅅ

standing

ㅇ
silent

The consonant **ㅇ** is silent at the beginning of a syllable, and pronounced **ng** at the end of a syllable.

✍ Practice writing ㅇ

silent, speechless

ㅈ
j

The consonant **ㅈ** makes a soft **j** sound, as in *j*udge, but with a little more air in the **j** sound.

✍ Practice writing ㅈ

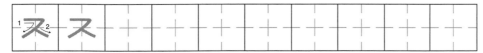

judge

SYLLABLES COMBINING THE BASIC CONSONANTS AND VOWELS

Now let's combine the consonants and vowels into syllables. Note that when consonants and vowels are combined, their shapes may change slightly from the shapes introduced on pages 8–11. Listen to the online audio recordings of each syllable, and write it using the grid lines to guide you.

Syllables Starting with the G Consonant ㄱ

가
ga

ㄱ + ㅏ = 가
g + a = ga

This combines the consonant ㄱ and the vowel ㅏ to make a syllable that has the sound **ga**.

✍ Practice writing 가

거
geo

ㄱ + ㅓ = 거
g + eo = geo

This combines the consonant ㄱ and the vowel ㅓ to make a syllable that has the sound **geo** (don't forget to round your lips!).

✍ Practice writing 거

기
gi

ㄱ + ㅣ = 기
g + i = gi

This combines the consonant ㄱ and the vowel ㅣ to make a syllable that has the sound **gi** (with a hard **g** sound).

✍ Practice writing 기

고	ㄱ + ㅗ = 고
go	g + o = go

This combines the consonant ㄱ and the vowel ㅗ to make a syllable that has the sound **go**.

✍ **Practice writing 고**

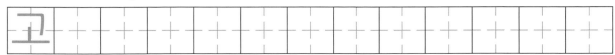

구	ㄱ + ㅜ = 구
gu	g + u = u

This combines the consonant ㄱ and the vowel ㅜ to make a syllable that has the sound **gu**.

✍ **Practice writing 구**

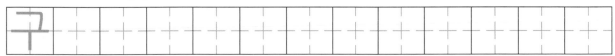

그	ㄱ + ㅡ = 그
geu	g + eu = geu

This combines the consonant ㄱ and the vowel ㅡ to make a syllable that has the sound **geu**.

✍ **Practice writing 그**

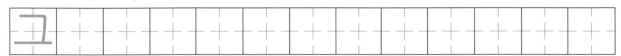

📖 **Reading Practice**

Underline the **g** syllable in the Hangeul word and write the pronunciation of the syllable. You can find the full romanized pronunciation of each word in the answer key on page 95.

1. vacation 휴<u>가</u> **ga**

2. cat 고양이 _____

3. picture 그림 _____

4. mood 기분 _____

5. there 거기 _____

6. furniture 가구 _____

Syllables Starting with the N Consonant

나 na	ㄴ + ㅏ = 나 n + a = na

This combines the consonant ㄴ and the vowel ㅏ to make a syllable that has the sound **na**.

✍️ Practice writing 나

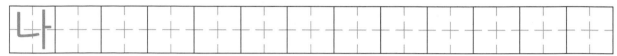

너 neo	ㄴ + ㅓ = 너 n + eo = neo

This combines the consonant ㄴ and the vowel ㅓ to make a syllable that has the sound **neo** (don't forget to round your lips!).

✍️ Practice writing 너

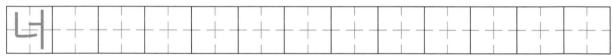

니 ni	ㄴ + ㅣ = 니 n + i = ni

This combines the consonant ㄴ and the vowel ㅣ to make a syllable that has the sound **ni**.

✍️ Practice writing 니

노 no	ㄴ + ㅗ = 노 n + o = no

This combines the consonant ㄴ and the vowel ㅗ to make a syllable that has the sound **no**.

✍️ Practice writing 노

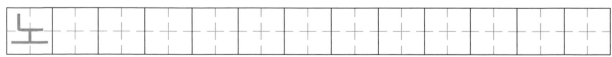

누
nu

ㄴ + ㅜ = 누
n + u = nu

This combines the consonant ㄴ and the vowel ㅜ to make a syllable that has the sound **nu**.

✍ **Practice writing 누**

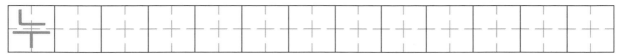

ㄴ
neu

ㄴ + ㅡ = ㄴ
n + eu = neu

This combines the consonant ㄴ and the vowel ㅡ to make a syllable that has the sound **neu**.

✍ **Practice writing ㄴ**

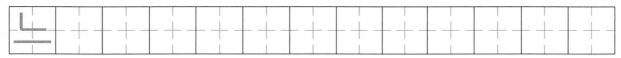

📖 **Reading Practice**

Underline the **n** syllable in the Hangeul word and write the pronunciation of the syllable. You can find the full romanized pronunciation of each word in the answer key on page 95.

1. too   너무   _____

2. feeling   느낌   _____

3. song   노래   _____

4. banana   바나나   _____

5. older sister 누나   _____

6. mother   어머니   _____

🎧 **Syllables Starting with the D Consonant** ㄷ

다
da

ㄷ + ㅏ = 다
d + a = da

This combines the consonant ㄷ and the vowel ㅏ to make a syllable that has the sound **da**.

✍ **Practice writing 다**

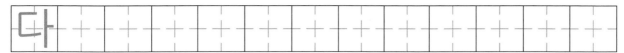

더	ㄷ + ㅓ = 더
deo	d + eo = deo

This combines the consonant ㄷ and the vowel ㅓ to make a syllable that has the sound **deo** (don't forget to round your lips!).

✍ **Practice writing 더**

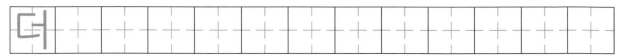

디	ㄷ + ㅣ = 디
di	d + i = di

This combines the consonant ㄷ and the vowel ㅣ to make a syllable that has the sound **di**.

✍ **Practice writing 디**

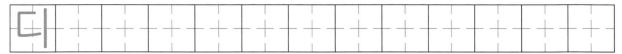

도	ㄷ + ㅗ = 도
do	d + o = do

This combines the consonant ㄷ and the vowel ㅗ to make a syllable that has the sound **do**.

✍ **Practice writing 도**

두	ㄷ + ㅜ = 두
du	d + u = du

This combines the consonant ㄷ and the vowel ㅜ to make a syllable that has the sound **du**.

✍ **Practice writing 두**

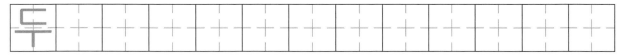

드 deu	ㄷ + ㅡ = 드 d + eu = deu

This combines the consonant ㄷ and the vowel ㅡ to make a syllable that has the sound **deu**.

✍ **Practice writing 드**

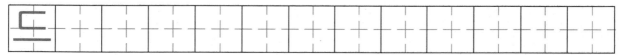

📖 **Reading Practice**

Underline the **d** syllable in the Hangeul word and write the pronunciation of the syllable. You can find the full romanized pronunciation of each word in the answer key on page 95.

1. radio   라디오   _____

2. leg   다리   _____

3. grapes   포도   _____

4. tofu   두부   _____

5. heat   더위   _____

6. drama   드라마   _____

🎧 Syllables Starting with the R Consonant ㄹ

라 ra	ㄹ + ㅏ = 라 r + a = ra

This combines the consonant ㄹ and the vowel ㅏ to make a syllable that has the sound **ra**.

✍ **Practice writing 라**

러 reo	ㄹ + ㅓ = 러 r + eo = reo

This combines the consonant ㄹ and the vowel ㅓ to make a syllable that has the sound **reo** (don't forget to round your lips!).

✍ **Practice writing 러**

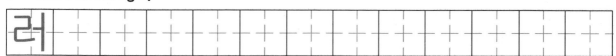

리
ri

ㄹ + ㅣ = 리
r + i = ri

This combines the consonant ㄹ and the vowel ㅣ to make a syllable that has the sound ri.

✍ **Practice writing 리**

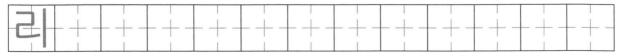

로
ro

ㄹ + ㅗ = 로
r + o = ro

This combines the consonant ㄹ and the vowel ㅗ to make a syllable that has the sound ro.

✍ **Practice writing 로**

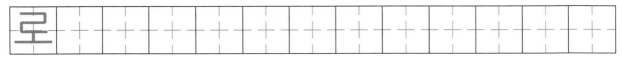

루
ru

ㄹ + ㅜ = 루
r + u = ru

This combines the consonant ㄹ and the vowel ㅜ to make a syllable that has the sound ru.

✍ **Practice writing 루**

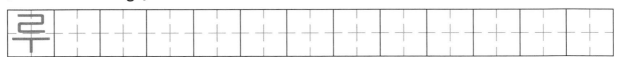

르
reu

ㄹ + ㅡ = 르
r + eu = reu

This combines the consonant ㄹ and the vowel ㅡ to make a syllable that has the sound reu.

✍ **Practice writing 르**

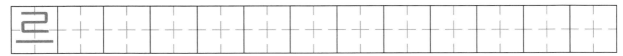

📖 Reading Practice

Underline the **r** syllable in the Hangeul word and write the pronunciation of the syllable. You can find the full romanized pronunciation of each word in the answer key on page 95.

1. road 도로 _____

2. day 하루 _____

3. dollar 달러 _____

4. ramyeon noodles 라면 _____

5. to choose 고르다 _____

6. head 머리 _____

🎧 Syllables Starting with the M Consonant ㅁ

마 ma	ㅁ + ㅏ = 마 m + a = ma

This combines the consonant ㅁ and the vowel ㅏ to make a syllable that has the sound **ma**.

✍ Practice writing 마

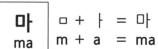

마												

머 meo	ㅁ + ㅓ = 머 m + eo = meo

This combines the consonant ㅁ and the vowel ㅓ to make a syllable that has the sound **meo**.

✍ Practice writing 머

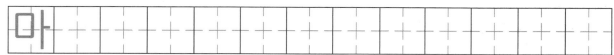

미 mi	ㅁ + ㅣ = 미 m + i = mi

This combines the consonant ㅁ and the vowel ㅣ to make a syllable that has the sound **mi**.

✍ Practice writing 미

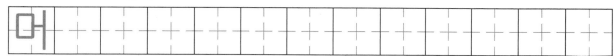

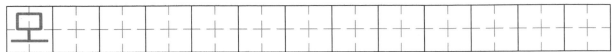

This combines the consonant ㅁ and the vowel ㅗ to make a syllable that has the sound **mo**.

✍ **Practice writing 모**

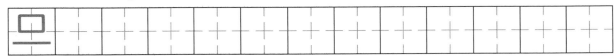

This combines the consonant ㅁ and the vowel ㅜ to make a syllable that has the sound **mu**.

✍ **Practice writing 무**

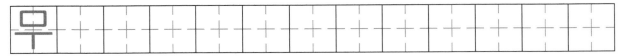

This combines the consonant ㅁ and the vowel ㅡ to make a syllable that has the sound **meu**.

✍ **Practice writing 므**

📖 **Reading Practice**

Underline the **m** syllable in the Hangeul word and write the pronunciation of the syllable. You can find the full romanized pronunciation of each word in the answer key on page 95.

1. hat   모자   _____   4. grandmother   할머니   _____

2. knee   무릎   _____   5. America   미국   _____

3. heart   마음   _____   6. omurice (rice omelet)   오므라이스 _____

The following words contain the syllables you have just learned. Listen to the audio recordings and practice pronouncing the words as you write them in the boxes provided.

거미   **geomi**   spider

거	미											

고구마   **goguma**   sweet potato

고	구	마									

고리   **gori**   chain

고	리											

너구리   **neoguri**   raccoon

너	구	리									

누나   **nuna**   older sister (of a boy)

누	나											

노루   **noru**   deer

노	루											

머리   **meori**   head

머	리											

고기   **gogi**   meat

고	기											

무기   **mugi**   weapon

무	기											

나무   **namu**   tree

나	무											

Syllables Starting with the B Consonant ㅂ

ㅂ + ㅏ = 바
b + a = ba

This combines the consonant ㅂ and the vowel ㅏ to make a syllable that has the sound **ba**.

✍ **Practice writing 바**

ㅂ + ㅓ = 버
b + eo = beo

This combines the consonant ㅂ and the vowel ㅓ to make a syllable that has the sound **beo** (don't forget to round your lips!).

✍ **Practice writing 버**

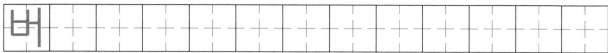

ㅂ + ㅣ = 비
b + i = bi

This combines the consonant ㅂ and the vowel ㅣ to make a syllable that has the sound **bi**.

✍ **Practice writing 비**

ㅂ + ㅗ = 보
b + o = bo

This combines the consonant ㅂ and the vowel ㅗ to make a syllable that has the sound **bo**.

✍ **Practice writing 보**

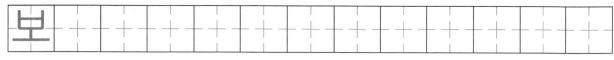

부	ㅂ + ㅜ = 부
bu	b + u = bu

This combines the consonant ㅂ and the vowel ㅜ to make a syllable that has the sound **bu**.

✍ **Practice writing 부**

부												

브	ㅂ + ─ = 브
beu	b + eu = beu

This combines the consonant ㅂ and the vowel ─ to make a syllable that has the sound **beu**.

✍ **Practice writing 브**

브												

📖 **Reading Practice**

Underline the **b** syllable in the Hangeul word and write the pronunciation of the syllable. You can find the full romanized pronunciation of each word in the answer key on page 95.

1. father   아버지 _____   4. ocean   바다 _____

2. study   공부 _____   5. plane   비행기 _____

3. TV   티브이 _____   6. idiot   바보 _____

🎧 ## Syllables Starting with the S Consonant ㅅ

사	ㅅ + ㅏ = 사
sa	s + a = sa

This combines the consonant ㅅ and the vowel ㅏ to make a syllable that has the sound **sa**.

✍ **Practice writing 사**

사												

서	ㅅ + ㅓ = 서
seo	s + eo = seo

This combines the consonant ㅅ and the vowel ㅓ to make a syllable that has the sound **seo** (don't forget to round your lips!).

✍️ **Practice writing 서**

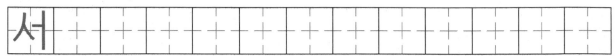

시	ㅅ + ㅣ = 시
si	s + i = si

When paired with the ㅣ vowel the consonant ㅅ takes on a sort of **sh** sound, so they combine to make a syllable that has the sound **shi**.

✍️ **Practice writing 시**

소	ㅅ + ㅗ = 소
so	s + o = so

This combines the consonant ㅅ and the vowel ㅗ to make a syllable that has the sound **so**.

✍️ **Practice writing 소**

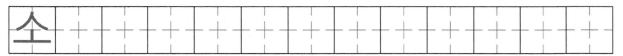

수	ㅅ + ㅜ = 수
su	s + u = su

This combines the consonant ㅅ and the vowel ㅜ to make a syllable that has the sound **su**.

✍️ **Practice writing 수**

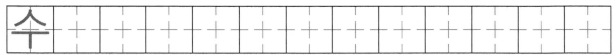

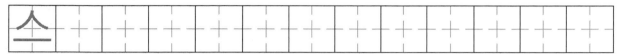

This combines the consonant ㅅ and the vowel ─ to make a syllable that has the sound **seu.**

✍️ **Practice writing 스**

스													

📖 **Reading Practice**

Underline the **s** syllable in the Hangeul word and write the pronunciation of the syllable. You can find the full romanized pronunciation of each word in the answer key on page 95.

1. time   시간   _____   4. singer   가수   _____

2. bus   버스   _____   5. apple   사과   _____

3. each other   서로   _____   6. address   주소   _____

🎧 **Syllables Starting with the Silent Consonant**

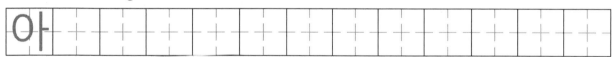

The consonant **o** is silent at the beginning of a syllable. It is attached to a vowel as a placeholder when that vowel needs to be pronounced by itself. The first combination is with the vowel sound ㅏ to make a syllable that has the sound **a.**

✍️ **Practice writing 아**

아													

This combines the silent consonant **o** and the vowel ㅓ to make a syllable that has the sound **eo** (don't forget to round your lips!).

✍️ **Practice writing 어**

어													

이
i

o + | = 이
silent + i = i

This combines the silent consonant o and the vowel | to make a syllable that has the sound i.

✍ **Practice writing 이**

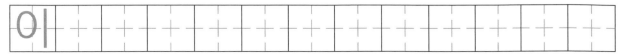

오
o

o + ⊥ = 오
silent + o = o

This combines the silent consonant o and the vowel ⊥ to make a syllable that has the sound o.

✍ **Practice writing 오**

우
u

o + ⊤ = 우
silent + u = u

This combines the silent consonant o and the vowel ⊤ to make a syllable that has the sound u.

✍ **Practice writing 우**

으
eu

o + — = 으
silent + eu = eu

This combines the silent consonant o and the vowel — to make a syllable that has the sound eu.

✍ **Practice writing 으**

📖 Reading Practice

Underline the silent consonant syllable in the Hangeul word and write the pronunciation of the syllable. You can find the full romanized pronunciation of each word in the answer key on page 95.

1. kid   유아   _____

2. yesterday   어제   _____

3. cucumber   오이   _____

4. best   으뜸   _____

5. us   우리   _____

6. today   오늘   _____

🎧 Syllables Starting with the J Consonant ㅈ

자
ja

ㅈ + ㅏ = 자
j + a = ja

This combines the consonant ㅈ and the vowel ㅏ to make a syllable that has the sound **ja**.

✍ Practice writing 자

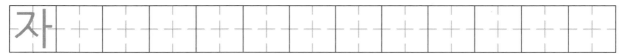

저
jeo

ㅈ + ㅓ = 저
j + eo = jeo

This combines the consonant ㅈ and the vowel ㅏ to make a syllable that has the sound **jeo** (don't forget to round your lips!).

✍ Practice writing 저

지
ji

ㅈ + ㅣ = 지
j + i = ji

This combines the consonant ㅈ and the vowel ㅣ to make a syllable that has the sound **ji**.

✍ Practice writing 지

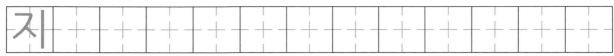

조
jo

ㅈ + ㅗ = 조
j + o = jo

This combines the consonant ㅈ and the vowel ㅗ to make a syllable that has the sound **jo**.

✍ **Practice writing 조**

조												

주
ju

ㅈ + ㅜ = 주
j + u = ju

This combines the consonant ㅈ and the vowel ㅜ to make a syllable that has the sound **ju**.

✍ **Practice writing 주**

주												

즈
jeu

ㅈ + ㅡ = 즈
j + eu = jeu

This combines the consonant ㅈ and the vowel ㅡ to make a syllable that has the sound **jeu**.

✍ **Practice writing 즈**

즈												

📖 **Reading Practice**

Underline the **j** syllable in the Hangeul word and write the pronunciation of the syllable. You can find the full romanized pronunciation of each word in the answer key on page 95.

1. often   자주   _____

2. dinner   저녁   _____

3. now   지금   _____

4. a little   조금   _____

5. very   아주   _____

6. cheese   치즈   _____

The following words contain the syllables you have just learned. Listen to the audio recordings and practice pronouncing the words as you write them in the boxes provided.

가수 **gasu** singer

가	수										

나비 **nabi** butterfly

나	비										

두더지 **dudeoji** mole

두	더	지								

소리 **sori** sound

소	리										

사다리 **sadari** ladder

사	다	리								

우주 **uju** universe

우	주										

지구 **jigu** earth

지	구										

버스 **beoseu** bus

버	스										

오이 **oi** cucumber

오	이										

우비 **ubi** raincoat

우	비										

SYLLABLES STARTING WITH ASPIRATED CONSONANTS

Korean has five aspirated consonants, pronounced with an extra breath added to the sound. Listen to the audio recordings and practice pronouncing the syllables as you write them in the boxes.

🎧 The Five Aspirated Consonants

ㅊ	ch	The consonant ㅊ is the aspirated version of ㅈ j. It makes a ch sound, as in *ch*icken.
ㅋ	k	The consonant ㅋ is the aspirated version of ㄱ g. It makes a k sound, as in *k*angaroo.
ㅌ	t	The consonant ㅌ is the aspirated version of ㄷ d. It makes a t sound, as in *t*icket.
ㅍ	p	The consonant ㅍ is the aspirated version of ㅂ b. It makes a p sound, as in *p*odium.
ㅎ	h	The consonant ㅎ is the aspirated version of ㅇ (silent). It makes an h sound, as in *h*at.

ㅊ
ch

The consonant ㅊ is the aspirated version of ㅈ. It makes a ch sound, as in chicken.

✍ **Practice writing ㅊ**

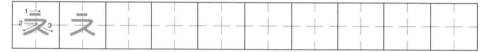

chicken

ㅋ
k

The consonant ㅋ is the aspirated version of ㄱ. It makes a k sound, as in kangaroo.

✍ **Practice writing ㅋ**

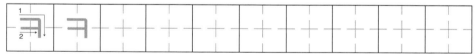

kangaroo

ㅌ
t

The consonant ㅌ is the aspirated version of ㄷ. It makes a t sound, as in ticket.

✍ **Practice writing ㅋ**

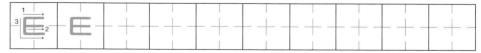

ticket

ㅍ p

The consonant **ㅍ** is the aspirated version of **ㅂ**. It makes a **p** sound, as in podium.

podium

👆 **Practice writing ㅍ**

ㅎ h

The consonant **ㅎ** is the aspirated version of **ㅇ**. It makes an **h** sound, as in hat

hat

👆 **Practice writing ㅋ**

🎧 Syllables Starting with the CH Consonant ㅊ

차 cha	ㅊ + ㅏ = 차 ch + a = cha

This combines the consonant **ㅊ** and the vowel **ㅏ** to make a syllable that has the sound **cha**.

✍ **Practice writing 차**

처 cheo	ㅊ + ㅓ = 처 ch + eo = cheo

This combines the consonant **ㅊ** and the vowel **ㅓ** to make a syllable that has the sound **cheo** (don't forget to round your lips!).

✍ **Practice writing 처**

치
chi

ㅊ + ㅣ = 치
ch + i = chi

This combines the consonant ㅊ and the vowel ㅣ to make a syllable that has the sound **chi**.

✍ **Practice writing 치**

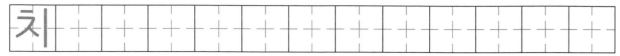

초
cho

ㅊ + ㅗ = 초
ch + o = cho

This combines the consonant ㅊ and the vowel ㅗ to make a syllable that has the sound **cho**.

✍ **Practice writing 초**

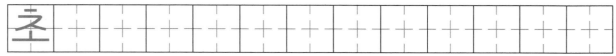

추
chu

ㅊ + ㅜ = 추
ch + u = chu

This combines the consonant ㅊ and the vowel ㅜ to make a syllable that has the sound **chu**.

✍ **Practice writing 추**

츠
cheu

ㅊ + ㅡ = 츠
ch + eu = cheu

This combines the consonant ㅊ and the vowel ㅡ to make a syllable that has the sound **cheu**.

✍ **Practice writing 츠**

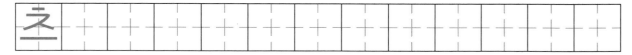

Reading Practice

Underline the **ch** syllable in the Hangeul word and write the pronunciation of the syllable. You can find the full romanized pronunciation of each word in the answer key on page 95.

1. invitation	초대	_____	4. pepper	고추	_____
2. sports	스포츠	_____	5. green tea	녹차	_____
3. for the first time	처음	_____	6. skirt	치마	_____

🎧 Syllables Starting with the K Consonant ㅋ

카
ka

ㅋ + ㅏ = 카
k + a = ka

This combines the consonant ㅋ and the vowel ㅏ to make a syllable that has the sound **ka**.

✍ Practice writing 카

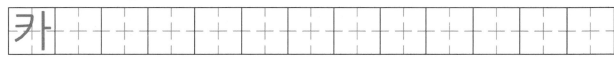

커
keo

ㅋ + ㅓ = 커
k + eo = keo

This combines the consonant ㅋ and the vowel ㅓ to make a syllable that has the sound **keo** (don't forget to round your lips!).

✍ Practice writing 커

키
ki

ㅋ + ㅣ = 키
k + i = ki

This combines the consonant ㅋ and the vowel ㅣ to make a syllable that has the sound **ki**.

✍ Practice writing 키

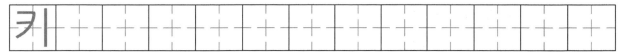

코 ko	ㅋ + ㅗ = 코 k + o = ko

This combines the consonant ㅋ and the vowel ㅗ to make a syllable that has the sound **ko**.

✍️ **Practice writing 코**

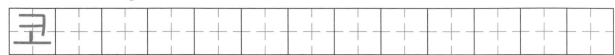

쿠 ku	ㅋ + ㅜ = 쿠 k + u = ku

This combines the consonant ㅋ and the vowel ㅜ to make a syllable that has the sound **ku**.

✍️ **Practice writing 쿠**

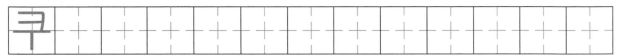

크 keu	ㅋ + ㅡ = 크 k + eu = keu

This combines the consonant ㅋ and the vowel ㅡ to make a syllable that has the sound **keu**.

✍️ **Practice writing 크**

📖 **Reading Practice**

Underline the **k** syllable in the Hangeul word and write the pronunciation of the syllable. You can find the full romanized pronunciation of each word in the answer key on page 95.

1. cookie 쿠키 _____ 4. ice cream 아이스크림 _____

2. card 카드 _____ 5. kiss 키스 _____

3. elephant 코끼리 _____ 6. coffee 커피 _____

타
ta

ㅌ + ㅏ = 타
t + a = ta

This combines the consonant ㅌ and the vowel ㅏ to make a syllable that has the sound **ta**.

✍️ **Practice writing 타**

터
teo

ㅌ + ㅓ = 터
t + eo = teo

This combines the consonant ㅌ and the vowel ㅓ to make a syllable that has the sound **teo** (don't forget to round your lips!).

✍️ **Practice writing 터**

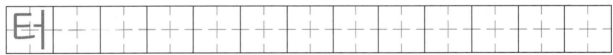

티
ti

ㅌ + ㅣ = 티
t + i = ti

This combines the consonant ㅌ and the vowel ㅣ to make a syllable that has the sound **ti**.

✍️ **Practice writing 티**

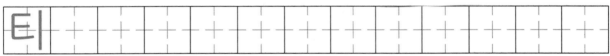

토
to

ㅌ + ㅗ = 토
t + o = to

This combines the consonant ㅌ and the vowel ㅗ to make a syllable that has the sound **to**.

✍️ **Practice writing 토**

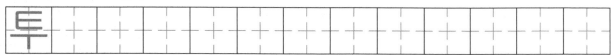

| 투
tu | ㅌ + ㅜ = 투
t + u = tu |

This combines the consonant ㅌ and the vowel ㅜ to make a syllable that has the sound **tu**.

✍️ **Practice writing 투**

| 트
teu | ㅌ + ― = 트
t + eu = teu |

This combines the consonant ㅌ and the vowel ― to make a syllable that has the sound **teu**.

✍️ **Practice writing 트**

📖 **Reading Practice**

Underline the **t** syllable in the Hangeul word and write the pronunciation of the syllable. You can find the full romanized pronunciation of each word in the answer key on page 95.

1. dialect   사투리   _____   4. computer   컴퓨터   _____

2. ticket   티켓   _____   5. style   스타일   _____

3. apartment   아파트   _____   6. rabbit   토끼   _____

🎧 Syllables Starting with the P Consonant ㅍ

| 파
pa | ㅍ + ㅏ = 파
p + a = pa |

This combines the consonant ㅍ and the vowel ㅏ to make a syllable that has the sound **pa**.

✍️ **Practice writing 파**

퍼 peo	ㅍ + ㅓ = 퍼 p + eo = peo

This combines the consonant ㅍ and the vowel ㅓ to make a syllable that has the sound **peo** (don't forget to round your lips!).

✍ **Practice writing 퍼**

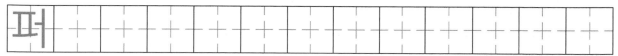

피 pi	ㅍ + ㅣ = 피 p + i = pi

This combines the consonant ㅍ and the vowel ㅣ to make a syllable that has the sound **pi**.

✍ **Practice writing 피**

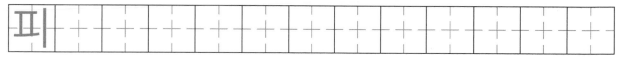

포 po	ㅍ + ㅗ = 포 p + o = po

This combines the consonant ㅍ and the vowel ㅗ to make a syllable that has the sound **po**.

✍ **Practice writing 포**

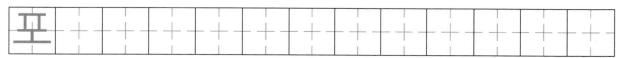

푸 pu	ㅍ + ㅜ = 푸 p + u = pu

This combines the consonant ㅍ and the vowel ㅜ to make a syllable that has the sound **pu**.

✍ **Practice writing 푸**

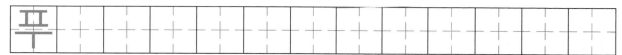

ㅍ	ㅍ + ㅡ = 프
peu	p + eu = peu

This combines the consonant **ㅍ** and the vowel **ㅡ** to make a syllable that has the sound **peu**.

✍ **Practice writing ㅍ**

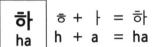

📖 **Reading Practice**

Underline the **p** syllable in the Hangeul word and write the pronunciation of the syllable. You can find the full romanized pronunciation of each word in the answer key on page 95.

1. France   프랑스 _____   4. pizza   피자 _____

2. shampoo   샴푸 _____   5. campus   캠퍼스 _____

3. fork   포크 _____   6. onion   양파 _____

🎧 Syllables Starting with the H Consonant ㅎ

하	ㅎ + ㅏ = 하
ha	h + a = ha

This combines the consonant **ㅎ** and the vowel **ㅏ** to make a syllable that has the sound **ha**.

✍ **Practice writing 하**

허	ㅎ + ㅓ = 허
heo	h + eo = heo

This combines the consonant **ㅎ** and the vowel **ㅓ** to make a syllable that has the sound **heo** (don't forget to round your lips!).

✍ **Practice writing 허**

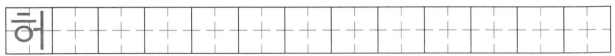

히	ㅎ + ㅣ = 히
hi	h + i = hi

This combines the consonant ㅎ and the vowel ㅣ to make a syllable that has the sound **hi**.

✍️ **Practice writing 히**

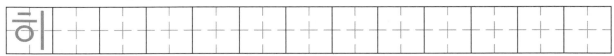

호	ㅎ + ㅗ = 호
ho	h + o = ho

This combines the consonant ㅎ and the vowel ㅗ to make a syllable that has the sound **ho**.

✍️ **Practice writing 호**

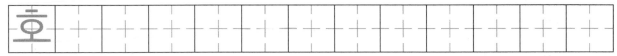

후	ㅎ + ㅜ = 후
hu	h + u = hu

This combines the consonant ㅎ and the vowel ㅜ to make a syllable that has the sound **hu**.

✍️ **Practice writing 후**

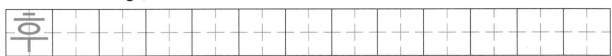

흐	ㅎ + ㅡ = 흐
heu	h + eu = heu

This combines the consonant ㅎ and the vowel ㅡ to make a syllable that has the sound **heu**.

✍️ **Practice writing 흐**

📖 **Reading Practice**

Underline the **h** syllable in the Hangeul word and write the pronunciation of the syllable. You can find the full romanized pronunciation of each word in the answer key on page 95.

1. junior   후배   _____   4. hijab   히잡   _____

2. flow   흐름   _____   5. number (phone)   번호   _____

3. one   하나   _____   6. waist   허리   _____

The following words contain syllables you have just learned. Listen to the audio recordings and practice pronouncing the words as you write them in the boxes provided.

기차 **gicha** train

기	차											

스키 **seuki** skiing

스	키											

키스 **kiseu** kiss

키	스											

지하 **jiha** basement

지	하											

피구 **pigu** dodgeball

피	구											

피자 **pija** pizza

피	자											

시트 **siteu** bedsheet

시	트											

마차 **macha** carriage

마	차											

모니터 **moniteo** monitor

모	니	터							

고추 **gochu** pepper

고	추											

하트 **hateu** heart

하	트												

추가 **chuga** addition

추	가												

카드 **kadeu** card

카	드												

하마 **hama** hippopotamus

하	마												

투자 **tuja** investment

투	자												

치마 **chima** skirt

치	마												

타자 **taja** typing

타	자												

기타 **gita** guitar

기	타												

차이 **chai** difference

차	이												

치아 **chia** tooth

치	아												

하루 **haru** day

하	루												

SYLLABLES STARTING WITH DOUBLE CONSONANTS

Korean also has five double consonants, formed by doubling other consonants to make a harder, sound. Practice pronunciation using the audio recordings and writing using the gridded boxes.

🎧 **The Five Double Consonants**

ㄲ gg The consonant ㄲ is the double version of ㄱ g. It makes a harder version of the g sound in *go*.

ㄸ dd The consonant ㄸ is the double version of ㄷ d. It makes a harder version of the d sound in *dog*.

ㅃ bb The consonant ㅃ is the double version of ㅂ b. It makes a harder version of the b sound in *boy*.

ㅆ ss The consonant ㅆ is the double version of ㅅ s. It makes a harder version of the s sound in *song*.

ㅉ jj The consonant ㅉ is the double version of ㅈ j. It makes a harder version of the j sound in *jog*.

✍ Practice writing ㄲ

✍ Practice writing ㄸ

✍ Practice writing ㅃ

✍ Practice writing ㅆ

✍ Practice writing ㅉ

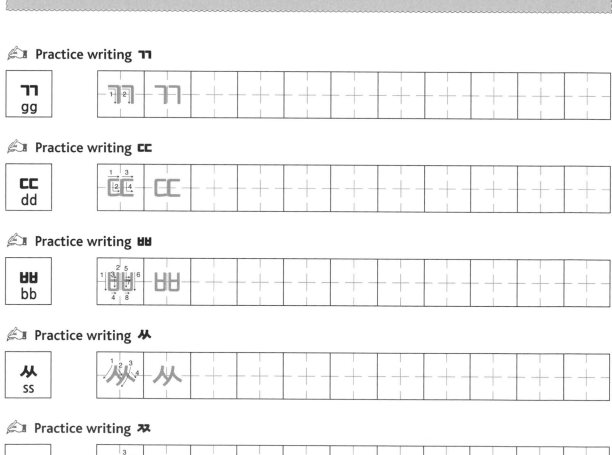

Syllables Starting with the GG Double Consonant ㄲ

까
gga

ㄲ + ㅏ = 까
gg + a = gga

This combines the consonant ㄲ and the vowel ㅏ to make a syllable that has the sound **gga**.

✍️ **Practice writing 까**

꺼
ggeo

ㄲ + ㅓ = 꺼
gg + eo = ggeo

This combines the consonant ㄲ and the vowel ㅓ to make a syllable that has the sound **ggeo**.

✍️ **Practice writing 꺼**

끼
ggi

ㄲ + ㅣ = 끼
gg + i = ggi

This combines the consonant ㄲ and the vowel ㅣ to make a syllable that has the sound **ggi**.

✍️ **Practice writing 끼**

꼬
ggo

ㄲ + ㅗ = 꼬
gg + o = ggo

This combines the consonant ㄲ and the vowel ㅗ to make a syllable that has the sound **ggo**.

✍️ **Practice writing 꼬**

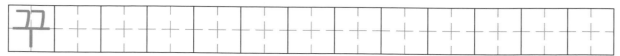

ꓩꓩ + ㅜ = 꾸
gg + u = ggu

ggu

This combines the consonant ꓩꓩ and the vowel ㅜ to make a syllable that has the sound **ggu**.

✍ **Practice writing 꾸**

ꓩꓩ + — = 끄
gg + eu = ggeu

ggeu

This combines the consonant ꓩꓩ and the vowel — to make a syllable that has the sound **ggeu**.

✍ **Practice writing 끄**

📖 **Reading Practice**

Underline the **gg** syllable in the Hangeul word and write the pronunciation of the syllable. You can find the full romanized pronunciation of each word in the answer key on page 95.

1. toad   두꺼비 _____   4. magpie   까치 _____

2. nodding   끄덕 _____   5. ax   도끼 _____

3. little kid   꼬마 _____   6. cuckoo   뻐꾸기 _____

🎧 **Syllables Starting with the DD Double Consonant** ㄸ

ㄸ + ㅏ = 따
dd + a = dda

dda

This combines the consonant ㄸ and the vowe ㅏ to make a syllable that has the sound **dda**.

✍ **Practice writing 따**

떠 ddeo	ㄸ + ㅓ = 떠 dd + eo = ddeo

This combines the consonant ㄸ and the vowel ㅓ to make a syllable that has the sound **ddeo** (don't forget to round your lips!).

✍️ **Practice writing 떠**

띠 ddi	ㄸ + ㅣ = 띠 dd + i = ddi

This combines the consonant ㄸ and the vowel ㅣ to make a syllable that has the sound **ddi**.

✍️ **Practice writing 띠**

또 ddo	ㄸ + ㅗ = 또 dd + o = ddo

This combines the consonant ㄸ and the vowel ㅗ to make a syllable that has the sound **ddo**.

✍️ **Practice writing 또**

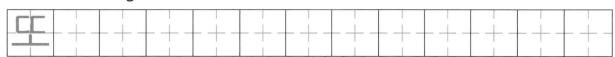

뚜 ddu	ㄸ + ㅜ = 뚜 dd + u = ddu

This combines the consonant ㄸ and the vowel ㅜ to make a syllable that has the sound **ddu**.

✍️ **Practice writing 뚜**

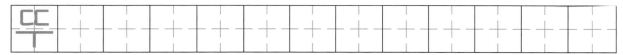

뜨 ddeu	ㄸ + ㅡ = 뜨 dd + eu = ddeu

This combines the consonant ㄸ and the vowel ㅡ to make a syllable that has the sound **ddeu**.

Practice writing 뜨

뜨												

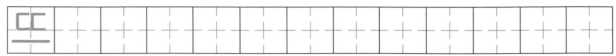

Reading Practice

Underline the **dd** syllable in the Hangeul word and write the pronunciation of the syllable. You can find the full romanized pronunciation of each word in the answer key on page 95.

1. in a while 이따 ________
2. the very best 으뜸 ________
3. belt 허리띠 ________
4. people of similar age 또래 ________
5. lid 뚜껑 ________
6. daughter (polite) 따님 ________

Syllables Starting with the BB Double Consonant ㅃ

빠 bba	ㅃ + ㅏ = 빠 bb + a = bba

This combines the consonant ㅃ and the vowel ㅏ to make a syllable that has the sound **bba**.

Practice writing 빠

빠												

뻐 bbeo	ㅃ + ㅓ = 뻐 bb + eo = bbeo

This combines the consonant ㅃ and the vowel ㅓ to make a syllable that has the sound **bbeo** (don't forget to round your lips!).

Practice writing 뻐

뻐												

빠	ㅃ + ㅣ = 빠
bbi	bb + i = bbi

This combines the consonant ㅃ and the vowel ㅣ to make a syllable that has the sound **bbi**.

✍ **Practice writing 빠**

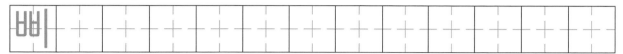

뽀	ㅃ + ㅗ = 뽀
bbo	bb + o = bbo

This combines the consonant ㅃ and the vowel ㅗ to make a syllable that has the sound **bbo**.

✍ **Practice writing 뽀**

뿌	ㅃ + ㅜ = 뿌
bbu	bb + u = bbu

This combines the consonant ㅃ and the vowel ㅜ to make a syllable that has the sound **bbu**.

✍ **Practice writing 뿌**

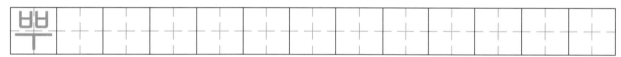

쁘	ㅃ + ― = 쁘
bbeu	bb + eu = bbeu

This combines the consonant ㅃ and the vowel ― to make a syllable that has the sound **bbeu**.

✍ **Practice writing 쁘**

📖 **Reading Practice**

Underline the **bb** syllable in the Hangeul word and write the pronunciation of the syllable. You can find the full romanized pronunciation of each word in the answer key on page 95.

1. roots   뿌리 _____   4. kiss   뽀뽀 _____

2. cuckoo   뻐꾸기 _____   5. older brother (of a girl)   오빠 _____

3. pager   삐삐 _____   6. petite   쁘띠 _____

🎧 Syllables Starting with the SS Double Consonant ㅆ

| 싸 ssa | ㅆ + ㅏ = 싸
ss + a = ssa |

This combines the consonant ㅆ and the vowel ㅏ to make a syllable that has the sound **ssa**.

✍ **Practice writing 싸**

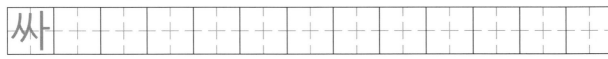

| 써 sseo | ㅆ + ㅓ = 써
ss + eo = sseo |

This combines the consonant ㅆ and the vowel ㅓ to make a syllable that has the sound **sseo** (don't forget to round your lips!).

✍ **Practice writing 써**

| 씨 sshi | ㅆ + ㅣ = 씨
ss + i = sshi |

Like ㅅ, when paired with the ㅣ vowel, the ㅆ takes on a hard **sh** sound, so they combine to make a syllable that has the sound **sshi**.

✍ **Practice writing 씨**

쏘	쏘 + ㅗ = 쏘
sso	ss + o = sso

This combines the consonant **ㅆ** and the vowel **ㅗ** to make a syllable that has the sound **sso**.

✍️ **Practice writing 쏘**

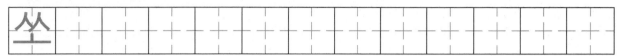

쑤	쑤 + ㅜ = 쑤
ssu	ss + u = ssu

This combines the consonant **ㅆ** and the vowel **ㅜ** to make a syllable that has the sound **ssu**.

✍️ **Practice writing 쑤**

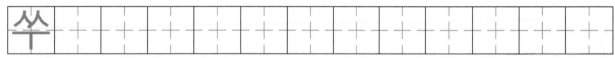

쓰	쓰 + ㅡ = 쓰
sseu	ss + eu = sseu

This combines the consonant **ㅆ** and the vowel **ㅡ** to make a syllable that has the sound **sseu**.

✍️ **Practice writing 쓰**

📖 **Reading Practice**

Underline the **ss** syllable in the Hangeul word and write the pronunciation of the syllable. You can find the full romanized pronunciation of each word in the answer key on page 95.

1. fight   싸움   _____

2. a common occurence 일쑤   _____

3. mandarin fish   쏘가리   _____

4. already   벌써   _____

5. weather   날씨   _____

6. trash   쓰레기   _____

🎧 Syllables Starting with the JJ Double Consonant ㅉ

짜	ㅉ + ㅏ = 짜
jja	jj + a = jja

This combines the consonant ㅉ and the vowel ㅏ to make a syllable that has the sound **jja**.

✍ Practice writing 짜

쩌	ㅉ + ㅓ = 쩌
jjeo	jj + eo = jjeo

This combines the consonant ㅉ and the vowel ㅓ to make a syllable that has the sound **jjeo** (don't forget to round your lips!).

✍ Practice writing 쩌

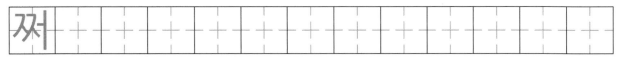

찌	ㅉ + ㅣ = 찌
jji	jj + i = jji

This combines the consonant ㅉ and the vowel ㅣ to make a syllable that has the sound **jji**.

✍ Practice writing 찌

쪼	ㅉ + ㅗ = 쪼
jjo	jj + o = jjo

This combines the consonant ㅉ and the vowel ㅗ to make a syllable that has the sound **jjo**.

✍ Practice writing 쪼

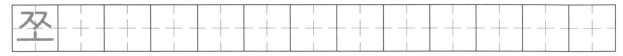

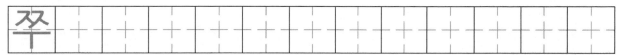

쭈
jju | ㅉ + ㅜ = 쭈
jj + u = jju

This combines the consonant ㅉ and the vowel ㅜ to make a syllable that has the sound **jju**.

✍ **Practice writing 쭈**

쭈												

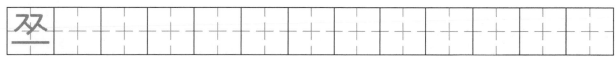

쯔
jjeu | ㅉ + ㅡ = 쯔
jj + eu = jjeu

This combines the consonant ㅉ and the vowel ㅡ to make a syllable that has the sound **jjeu**.

✍ **Practice writing 쯔**

쯔												

📖 **Reading Practice**

Underline the jj syllable in the Hangeul word and write the pronunciation of the syllable. You can find the full romanized pronunciation of each word in the answer key on page 95.

1. tsuyu dipping sauce   쯔유 _____

2. free   공짜 _____

3. wrinkled   쭈글쭈글 _____

4. stew   찌개 _____

COMPLEX VOWELS

The six basic vowels introduced on pages 8–9 can be combined to make more complex vowel sounds. These complex sounds consist of nine diphthongs (two vowels that are combined to make a new sound) and six vowels that we refer to here as the Y sounds. Letters having the Y sound are created by adding an extra line to six existing vowels and diphthongs. Listen to the online audio recordings and practice pronouncing the vowels as you write them in the boxes provided.

🎧 The Nine Diphthongs

ㅐ **ae** We can combine the vowels ㅏ and ㅣ to make the diphthong ㅐ ae. This makes the sound **ay**, as in p**a**y or m**a**y.

ㅔ **e** We can combine the vowels ㅓ and ㅣ to make the diphthong ㅔ e. This also makes the sound **ay**, as in p**a**y or m**a**y.

ㅘ **wa** We can combine the vowels ㅗ and ㅏ to make the diphthong ㅘ wa. This makes the sound **wa**, as in **wa**ter (in American English).

ㅚ **oe** We can combine the vowels ㅗ and ㅣ to make the diphthong ㅚ oe. This makes the sound **way**, as in w**ei**gh.

ㅙ **wae** We can combine the vowels ㅗ and ㅐ to make the diphthong ㅙ wae. This also makes the sound **way**, as in w**ei**gh.

ㅝ **wo** We can combine the vowels ㅜ and ㅓ to make the diphthong ㅝ wo. This makes the sound **wo**, as in **wo**nder.

ㅞ **we** We can combine the vowels ㅜ and ㅔ to make the diphthong ㅞ we. This also makes the sound **way**, as in w**ei**gh.

ㅟ **wi** We can combine the vowels ㅜ and ㅣ to make the diphthong ㅟ wi. This makes the sound **wee**, as in the word **we**.

ㅢ **ui** We can combine the vowels ㅡ and ㅣ to make the diphthong ㅢ ui. This literally combines the **u** sound of ㅡ and the **ee** sound of ㅣ to make the sound **ui**, as in the French word for yes.

🎧 The Six Y Sounds

ㅑ **ya** Add a line to the basic vowel ㅏ a so it becomes ㅑ ya.

ㅕ **yeo** Add a line to the basic vowel ㅓ eo so it becomes ㅕ yeo.

ㅛ **yo** Add a line to the basic vowel ㅗ o so it becomes ㅛ yo.

ㅠ **yu** Add a line to the basic vowel ㅜ u so it becomes ㅠ yu.

ㅒ **yae** Add a line to the diphthong ㅐ ae so it becomes ㅒ yae.

ㅖ **yee** Add a line to the diphthong ㅔ e so it becomes ㅖ ye.

✍ Practice writing ㅐ ae

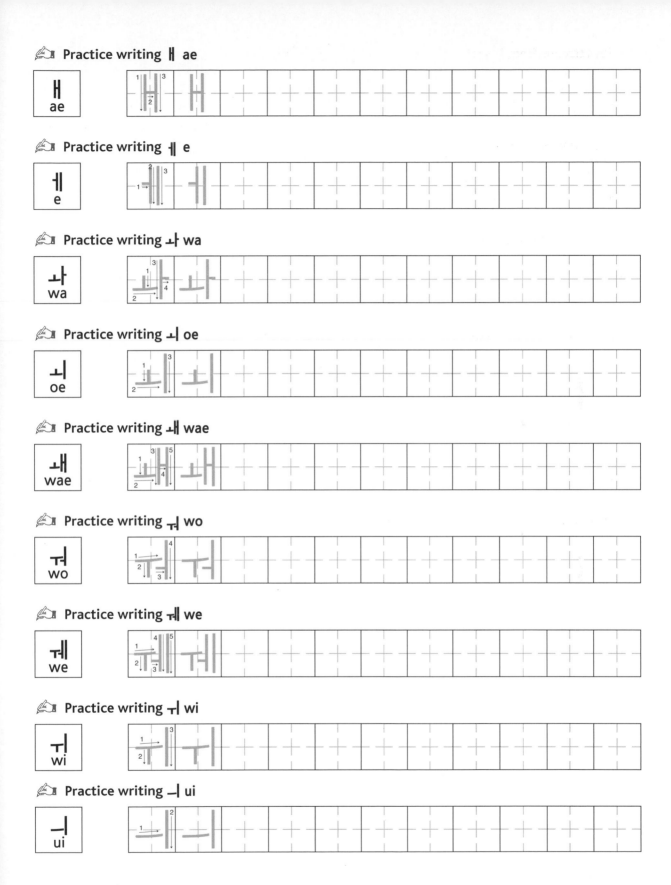

✍ Practice writing ㅔ e

✍ Practice writing ㅘ wa

✍ Practice writing ㅚ oe

✍ Practice writing ㅙ wae

✍ Practice writing ㅝ wo

✍ Practice writing ㅞ we

✍ Practice writing ㅟ wi

✍ Practice writing ㅢ ui

✍ Practice writing ㅑ ya

✍ Practice writing ㅕ yeo

✍ Practice writing ㅛ yo

✍ Practice writing ㅠ yu

✍ Practice writing ㅒ yae

✍ Practice writing ㅖ ye

Just like the six basic vowels, complex vowels combine with various consonants to create different syllable sounds. For example, if we add a ㄱ g consonant to the ㅟ wi complex vowel, they combine to form the syllable 귀 gwi. If we add a ㄴ n consonant to the ㅘ wa complex vowel, they combine to form the syllable 놔 nwa. Below are some examples of these combinations. See if you can write the romanized sound the new syllable will make. Find the answers on page 95. Then practice the pronunciation of each combination using the online audio recordings.

1.	뱌 _____		16.	뮈 _____
2.	겨 _____		17.	뷔 _____
3.	료 _____		18.	갸 _____
4.	뮤 _____		19.	뢔 _____
5.	대 _____		20.	뇨 _____
6.	얘 _____		21.	새 _____
7.	네 _____		22.	뒈 _____
8.	혜 _____		23.	유 _____
9.	과 _____		24.	죠 _____
10.	푀 _____		25.	혀 _____
11.	쇄 _____		26.	내 _____
12.	퉈 _____		27.	킈 _____
13.	줴 _____		28.	체 _____
14.	위 _____		29.	외 _____
15.	최 _____		30.	폐 _____

The following words include the complex vowel syllables you have just learned. Listen to the audio recordings and practice pronouncing the words as you write them in the boxes provided.

가게 **gage** shop

가	게													

가위 **gawi** scissors

가	위													

교사 **gyosa** teacher

교	사													

돼지 **dwaeji** pig

돼	지													

의자 **uija** chair

의	자													

귀뚜라미 **gwiddurami** cricket

귀	뚜	라	미									

유리 **yuri** glass

유	리													

위스키 **wiseuki** whisky

위	스	키									

휴지 **hyuji** toilet paper

휴	지													

야구 **yagu** baseball

야	구													

외모 **oemo** outer appearance

외	모												

파워 **pawo** power

파	워												

바위 **bawi** large rock

바	위												

기와 **giwa** traditional Korean roof tiles

기	와												

새 **sae** bird

새													

여자 **yeoja** woman

여	자												

얘기 **yaegi** story/talking (casual)

얘	기												

예의 **yeui** etiquette

예	의												

신뢰 **sinroe** trust

신	뢰												

의사 **uisa** doctor

의	사												

교수 **gyosu** professor

교	수												

케이크 **keikeu** cake

케	이	크								

FINAL CONSONANTS

We've looked at consonants at the beginning of syllables. Now we will practice adding consonants to the end of syllables.

Final consonants are always written at the bottom of the syllable as shown in the following writing practice exercise. The example syllables in this section aren't necessarily words by themselves, but they are often found in other words and phrases.

ㄱ
k

At the end of a syllable, ㄱ makes a soft **k** sound, as in lo*ck* or ca*ke* in English. Practice writing the following two syllables:

약   yak

복   bok

Note the final **k** in both syllables of the Korean word 축복 chukbok (blessing).

ㄴ
n

At the end of a syllable, ㄴ makes an **n** sound, as in ru*n* or ma*n*. Practice writing the following two syllables:

눈   nun

순   sun

Note the final **n** in the first syllable of the word 선생님 seonsaengnim (teacher).

ㄷ
t

At the end of a syllable, ㄷ makes a soft **t** sound, as in ha*t* or ho*t*. You won't actually pronounce the **t**, rather let your tongue stop before letting the **t** sound out. Practice writing the following two syllables:

맏   mat

돋   dot

Note the final **t** in the first syllable of the word 맏아들 matadeul (oldest son).

ㄹ
l

At the end of a syllable, ㄹ makes an l sound, as in ha*ll* or sma*ll*. Your tongue will be closer to the middle of the roof of your mouth than for the English letter *l*. Practice writing the following two syllables:

벌   beol

벌

굴   gul

굴

Note the final l in both syllables of the word 얼굴 **eolgul** (face).

ㅁ
m

At the end of a syllable, ㅁ makes an m sound, as in hi*m* or ja*m*. Practice writing the following two syllables:

암   am

암

봄   bom

봄

Note the final m in the word 암 **am** (cancer).

ㅂ
p

At the end of a syllable, ㅂ makes a p sound, as in sla*p* or to*p*. You won't actually pronounce the p, rather let your lips stop before letting the p sound out. Practice writing the following two syllables:

집   jip

집

즙   jeup

즙

Note the final p in the word 집 **jip** (home).

ㅅ
t

At the end of a syllable, ㅅ makes a soft t sound, as in ha*t* or ho*t*. You won't actually pronounce the t, rather let your tongue stop before letting the t sound out. Practice writing the following two syllables:

맛   mat

맛

곳   got

곳

Note the final t in the word 곳 **got** (place).

ㅇ ng

At the end of a syllable, **ㅇ** makes an **ng** sound, as in so*ng* or thi*ng*. Practice writing the following two syllables:

잉　　ing

등　　deung

Note the final ng in the word **전등** jeondeung (lamp).

ㅈ t

At the end of a syllable, **ㅈ** makes a soft **t** sound, as in ha*t* or ho*t*. You won't actually pronounce the **t**, rather let your tongue stop before letting the **t** sound out. Practice writing the following two syllables:

낮　　nat

궂　　gut

Note the final **t** in the word **낮** nat (day time).

ㅊ t

At the end of a syllable, **ㅊ** makes a soft **t** sound, as in ha*t* or ho*t*. You won't actually pronounce the **t**, rather let your tongue stop before letting the **t** sound out. Practice writing the following two syllables:

빛　　bit

꽃　　ggot

Note the final **t** in the word **햇빛** haetbit (sunlight).

ㅋ k

At the end of a syllable, **ㅋ** makes a soft **k** sound, as in lo*ck* or ca*ke*. Practice writing the following two syllables:

억　　eok

윽　　euk

Note the final **k** sound in the word **부엌** bueok (kitchen).

ㅌ	At the end of a syllable, ㅌ makes a soft **t** sound, as in ha*t* or ho*t*. You won't actually pronounce the **t**, rather let your tongue stop before letting the t sound out. Practice writing the following two syllables:
t	

밭 bat

밭

뭍 mut

뭍

Note the final **t** sound in the word **밭** bat (fields).

ㅍ	At the end of a syllable, ㅍ makes a **p** sound, as in sla*p* or to*p*. You won't actually pronounce the **p**, rather let your lips stop before letting the **p** sound out. Practice writing the following two syllables:
p	

잎 ip

잎

읖 eup

읖

Note the final p sound in the word **나뭇잎** namunnip (leaf).

ㅎ	At the end of a syllable, ㅎ makes a soft **t** sound, as in ha*t* or ho*t*. You won't actually pronounce the **t**, rather let your tongue stop before letting the **t** sound out. Practice writing the following two syllables:
t	

낳 nat

낳

놓 not

놓

Note the use of the syllable with the silent **t** sound in the word **낳다** nahta (to give birth).

ㄲ	At the end of a syllable, ㄲ makes a soft **k** sound, as in loc*k* or ca*ke*. Practice writing the following two syllables:
k	

닭 dak

닭

묶 muk

묶

Note the use of the final k sound in the word **묶음** mukkeum (bundle).

<table>
<tr><td>ㅆ
t</td><td>At the end of a syllable, **ㅆ** makes a soft **t** sound, as in ha*t* or ho*t*. You won't actually pronounce the **t**, rather let your tongue stop before letting the **t** sound out. Practice writing the following two syllables:</td></tr>
</table>

었 eot

았 at

This syllable is only used in the formation of the past tense of certain verbs.

The other double consonants **ㄸ dd**, **ㅃ bb**, and **ㅉ jj** don't usually appear at the end of a syllable.

Consonant Clusters at the End of a Syllable

Sometimes consonants appear in clusters of two at the end of a syllable. The following are some examples of what syllables with final consonant clusters look like. Write down the romanized form of each syllable. The first two have been done for you. Find the answers on page 96.

I.   삶 **salm**

2.   밟 **balp**

3.   읽 _____

4.   붉 _____

5.   꿇 _____

6.   앉 _____

7.   몫 _____

8.   핥 _____

9.   흙 _____

IO.   꿇 _____

The following words contain the syllables you have learned. Listen to the audio recordings and practice pronouncing the words as you write them in the boxes provided.

가방　**gabang**　bag

가	방														

가을　**gaeul**　autumn

가	을														

가족　**gajok**　family

가	족														

감기　**gamgi**　cold

감	기														

결혼　**gyeolhon**　marriage

결	혼														

날짜　**naljja**　date (on the calendar)

날	짜														

남편　**nampyeon**　husband

남	편														

닭고기　**dakgogi**　chicken meat

닭	고	기												

대학생　**daehaksaeng**　university student

대	학	생												

라면　**ramyeon**　Korean ramen noodles

라	면														

말씀 **malsseum** words

말	씀											

목욕 **mogyok** bath

목	욕											

미국 **miguk** America

미	국											

바람 **baram** wind

바	람											

병원 **byeongwon** hospital

병	원											

백화점 **baekwajeom** department store

백	화	점								

생각 **saenggak** thoughts

생	각											

선생님 **seonsaengnim** teacher

선	생	님								

슈퍼마켓 **syupeomaket** supermarket

슈	퍼	마	켓						

아들 **adeul** son

아	들											

아침 **achim** morning

아	침											

약속 **yaksok** promise

약	속													

얼굴 **eolgul** face

얼	굴													

영국 **yeongguk** England

영	국													

운동 **undong** exercise

운	동													

자동차 **jadongcha** car

자	동	차										

전화 **jeonhwa** telephone

전	화													

청소 **cheongso** cleaning

청	소													

칠판 **chilpan** blackboard

칠	판													

컴퓨터 **keompyuteo** computer

컴	퓨	터										

태권도 **taegwondo** taekwondo

태	권	도										

편지 **pyeonji** mail, letter

편	지													

한국말 **hangungmal** Korean (language)

한	국	말												

화장실 **hwajangsil** bathroom

화	장	실												

꽃잎 **ggotip** flower petals

꽃	잎													

땅콩 **ddangkong** peanut

땅	콩													

빵집 **bbangjip** bakery

빵	집													

싸움 **ssaum** fighting

싸	움													

쌀 **ssal** rice (uncooked)

쌀														

짜장면 **jjajangmyeon** black bean noodles

짜	장	면												

딸 **ddal** daughter

딸														

밥상 **babsang** table for eating

밥	상													

공책 **gongchaek** notebook

공	책													

PART TWO

Reading and Writing Practice

In this part of the book you'll find a variety of reading and writing exercises that will reinforce and consolidate your knowledge of the Korean alphabet. The sections are divided into useful everyday topics, ranging from daily expressions, numbers, family and food to K-pop, social media and IT.

• DAILY EXPRESSIONS •

Learn how to read, write and pronounce these useful daily expressions.

🎧 **GUIDED WRITING PRACTICE**
Practice writing each of the following words in the boxes provided.

안녕하세요　**annyeonghaseyo**　good morning (polite)

안	녕	하	세	요										

안녕　**annyeong**　hello (casual)

안	녕													

잘자요　**jal jayo**　good night

잘	자	요												

부탁해요　**butakhaeyo**　please

부	탁	해	요											

고맙습니다　**gomapseumnida**　thank you

고	맙	습	니	다									

미안합니다　**mianhamnida**　I'm sorry

미	안	합	니	다									

잘가요　**jal gayo**　goodbye

잘	가	요												

이름이 뭐예요　**Ireumi mwoyeyo?**　What's your name?

이	름	이	뭐	예	요									

내 이름은　**Nae ireumeun . . .**　My name is . . .

내	이	름	은											

어떻게 지내세요　**Eoddeoke jinaeseyo?**　How are you?

어	떻	게	지	내	세	요							

잘 지내요　**Jal Jinaeyo.**　I'm fine.

잘	지	내	요											

• NUMBERS •

Korean uses both Chinese and native Korean numbers. Chinese numbers are used when counting or talking about the numbers themselves (e.g., in maths or for temperatures, miles, etc.). Korean numbers are typically used when talking about quantities of people or things.

🎧 **GUIDED WRITING PRACTICE**
Practice writing each of the following words in the boxes provided.

✍ **The Chinese Numbers**

일 **il** one

일			

이 **i** two

이			

삼 **sam** three

삼			

사 **sa** four

사			

오 **o** five

오			

육 **yuk** six

육			

칠 **chil** seven

칠			

팔 **pal** eight

칠			

구 **gu** nine

구			

십 **sip** ten

십			

✍ **The Korean Numbers**

하나 **hana** one

하	나				

둘 **dul** two

둘					

셋 **set** three

셋					

넷 **net** four

넷					

다섯 **daseot** five

다	섯				

여섯 **yeoseot** six

여	섯				

일곱 **ilgop** seven

일	곱				

여덟 **yeodeol** eight

여	덟				

아홉 **ahop** nine

아	홉				

열 **yeol** ten

열					

📖 Reading Practice

Draw lines to match the English word with the Korean word. Practice sounding out the Korean as you go. Check your answers on page 96.

Chinese numbers

one	a) 칠		
two	b) 삼		
three	c) 오		
four	d) 일		
five	e) 십		
six	f) 구		
seven	g) 이		
eight	h) 육		
nine	i) 팔		
ten	j) 사		

Korean numbers

one	a) 여덟
two	b) 둘
three	c) 다섯
four	d) 하나
five	e) 셋
six	f) 일곱
seven	g) 넷
eight	h) 열
nine	i) 여섯
ten	j) 아홉

🎧 Listening and Reading Practice

Read and listen to the sentences below and underline the number word. Check your answers on page 96.

1. 아이들이 여덟 명 있었어.   They had eight children.

2. 이 년이 걸렸어요.   It took her two years.

3. 그가 고양이 열 마리를 봤어요.   He saw ten cats.

4. 다섯 시간 걸릴 거야.   That will take five hours.

5. 사과 여섯 개 주세요.   Please give me six apples.

6. 삼 일 동안 잤어요.   I slept for three days.

7. 구 페이지에 있어요.   It's on page nine.

8. 그녀의 집이 사 층에 있어요.   Her home is on the fourth floor.

9. 칠 일이 있었어요.   There were seven days.

10. 그는 일 번을 봤어요.   He looked at number one.

• COLORS •

🎧 **GUIDED WRITING PRACTICE**

Practice writing each of the following words in the boxes provided.

빨간색 **bbalgansaek**   red

| 빨 | 간 | 색 | | | | | | | | | | | | | |

파란색 **paransaek**   blue

| 파 | 란 | 색 | | | | | | | | | | | | | |

노란색 **noransaek**   yellow

| 노 | 란 | 색 | | | | | | | | | | | | | |

보라색 **borasaek**   purple

| 보 | 라 | 색 | | | | | | | | | | | | | |

초록색 **choroksaek**   green

| 초 | 록 | 색 | | | | | | | | | | | | | |

주황색 **juhwangsaek**   orange

| 주 | 황 | 색 | | | | | | | | | | | | | |

하얀색 **hayansaek**   white

| 하 | 얀 | 색 | | | | | | | | | | | | | |

검정색 **geomjeongsaek**   black

| 검 | 정 | 색 | | | | | | | | | | | | | |

회색 **hoesaek**   gray

| 회 | 색 | | | | | | | | | | | | | | | |

분홍색 **bunhongsaek**   pink

| 분 | 홍 | 색 | | | | | | | | | | | | | |

하늘색 **haneulsaek**   sky blue

| 하 | 늘 | 색 | | | | | | | | | | | | | |

📖 Reading Practice

Draw lines to match the English word with the Korean word. Practice sounding out the Korean as you go. Check your answers on page 96.

1. 하얀색   a) black

2. 노란색   b) gray

3. 파란색   c) blue

4. 회색   d) yellow

5. 초록색   e) purple

6. 검정색   f) orange

7. 빨간색   g) red

8. 주황색   h) white

9. 보라색   i) green

🎧 Listening and Reading Practice

Read and listen to the sentences below, underline the Korean color word, and write the English color word into the gap. Check your answers on page 96.

1. 우리집 정원에 빨간색, 노란색 그리고 보라색 꽃이 있어요. There are _____ ,

   _____ and _____ flowers in my garden.

2. 그녀는 빨간색 옷을 자주 입었어. She often wore _____ clothes.

3. 검정색 양복을입고 왔어요. I came wearing a _____ suit.

4. 미국 사람 중에 눈이 파란색인 사람이 많아요. There are a lot of Americans with _____ eyes.

5. 보라색 동물은 없을 거야. There probably aren't any _____ animals.

6. 우리 아버지가 초록색 자동차를 샀어요. My father bought a _____ car.

7. 하얀색 구름이 정말 예뻤어. The _____ clouds were really beautiful.

8. 내 교복은 회색이에요. My school uniform is _____ .

9. 주황색은 행복해 보이는 색깔입니다. _____ is a cheerful color.

10. 내가 가장 좋아하는 색깔은 노란색이에요. My favorite color is _____.

🎧 GUIDED WRITING PRACTICE

Practice writing each of the following words in the boxes provided.

누나 **nuna** older sister (of a boy)

누	나												

언니 **eonni** older sister (of a girl)

언	니												

오빠 **obba** older brother (of a girl)

오	빠												

형 **hyeong** older brother (of a boy)

형													

동생 **dongsaeng** younger sibling

동	생												

아버지 **abeoji** father

아	버	지									

어머니 **eomeoni** mother

어	머	니									

할머니 **halmeoni** grandmother

할	머	니									

할아버지 **harabeoji** grandfather

할	아	버	지						

삼촌 **samchon** uncle

삼	촌												

숙모 **sungmo** uncle's wife

이	모														

사촌 **sachon** cousin

사	촌														

✎ Reading and Writing Practice

This is Minsu's family. Write the relationship of everyone to Minsu, choosing from the words below. Find the answers on page 96.

A) 숙모   B) 어머니   C) 할아버지   D) 아버지

E) 삼촌   F) 사촌   G) 할머니   H) 오빠

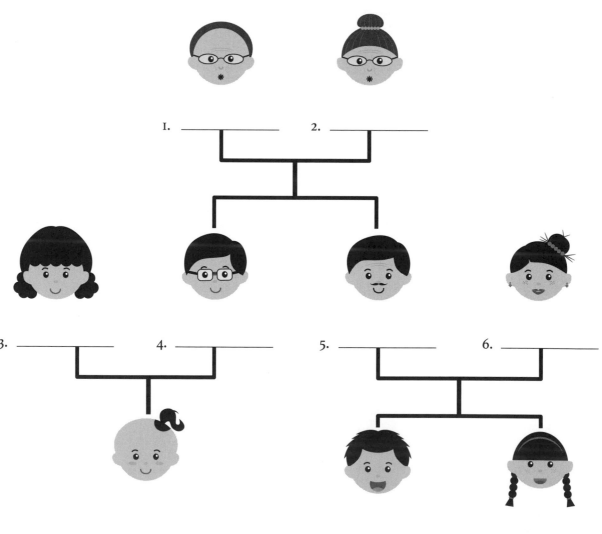

• FOODS •

Practice writing each of the following words in the boxes provided.

김치　**gimchi**　kimchi

김	치											

밥　**bap**　rice (cooked)

밥												

반찬　**banchan**　side dish

반	찬											

도시락　**dosirak**　lunchbox

도	시	락									

비빔밥　**bibimbap**　bibimbap

비	빔	밥									

불고기　**bulgogi**　bulgogi

불	고	기									

김밥　**gimbap**　kimbap

김	밥											

떡볶이　**ddeokbokki**　spicy rice cakes

떡	볶	이									

치킨　**chikin**　fried chicken

치	킨											

맥주　**maekju**　beer

맥	주											

치맥　**chimaek**　fried chicken and beer

치	맥											

삼겹살　**samgyeopsal**　pork belly

삼	겹	살									

사과　**sagwa**　apple

사	과											

복숭아　**boksunga**　peach

복	숭	아									

귤　**gyul**　mandarin orange

귤														

감　**gam**　persimmon

감														

배　**bae**　pear

배														

수박　**subak**　watermelon

수	박											

소주　**soju**　soju (Korean alcohol)

소	주											

국　**guk**　soup

국														

쌀　**ssal**　rice (uncooked)

쌀														

Look at the menu and answer the questions below. Check your answers on page 96.

한식당 메뉴

밥종류

비빔밥	8,000
볶음밥	6,000
떡볶이	6,000
김밥	4,000

고기

매운 맛 치킨	10,000
간장 치킨	10,000
돈까스	8,000
삼겹살	12,000

반찬

김치
콩나물
감자 조림
깍두기
오이 김치

주류

콜라	2,000
사이다	1,500
맥주	5,000
와인	10,000
소주	5,000

🔔 **Questions**

1. Write the names of the four rice dishes on the menu in English.

_____   _____

_____   _____

2. How many fried chicken dishes are on the menu?

_____

3. Write the name of the most expensive dish on the menu in English.

_____

4. How much is a beer?

_____

5. How many side dishes are on the menu?

_____

🎧 **Listening and Reading Practice**

Underline the food words in the following dialogue. Check your answers on page 96.

미나: 호빈아, 밥 먹으러 갈래?
Mina: Hobin, do you want to go for a meal?

호빈: 응. 김밥이나 떡볶이 먹자.
Hobin: Yes. Let's have kimbap or spicy rice cakes.

미나: 김밥은 싫어. 어제 먹었거든. 고기 어때? 불고기나 삼겹살이 땡기네.
Mina: I don't want kimbap. I had it yesterday. How about meat? I'm craving bulgogi or pork belly.

호빈: 고기는 비싸잖아. 그냥 치킨으로 할까?
Hobin: Meat is expensive though. Should we just get some fried chicken?

미나: 너무 좋아. 치킨 먹고 맥주 마시자.
Mina: That's great. Let's eat chicken and drink beer.

호빈: 좋지.
Hobin: Sounds good.

미나: 후식으로 우리 집에서 과일 먹자. 집에 맛있는 복숭아가 있거든.
Mina: For dessert let's go to my house and have fruit. I have tasty peaches at home.

• VERBS •

🎧 GUIDED WRITING PRACTICE

Practice writing each of the following verbs in the boxes provided.

하다 **hada** to do

하	다														

있다 **itda** to exist / to have

있	다														

자다 **jada** to sleep

자	다														

없다 **eopda** to not exist / to not have

없	다														

보다 **boda** to see

보	다														

주다 **juda** to give

주	다														

가다 **gada** to go

가	다														

공부하다 **gongbuhada** to study

공	부	하	다										

말하다 **malhada** to speak

말	하	다										

오다 **oda** to come

오	다														

알다 **alda** to know

알	다											

걷다 **geotda** to walk

걷	다											

따르다 **ddareuda** to follow

따	르	다							

살다 **salda** to live

살	다											

생각하다 **saenggakhada** to think

생	각	하	다					

만들다 **mandeulda** to make

만	들	다							

타다 **tada** to ride (a bicycle)

타	다											

먹다 **meokda** to eat

먹	다											

앉다 **anjda** to sit

앉	다											

서다 **seoda** to stand

서	다											

뛰다 **dduida** to run

뛰	다											

Reading Practice

Draw lines to match the English word with the Korean word. Practice sounding out the Korean as you go. Check your answers on page 96.

1. 앉다   a) to go

2. 보다   b) to sleep

3. 타다   c) to sit

4. 걷다   d) to ride

5. 자다   e) to stand

6. 오다   f) to see

7. 가다   g) to study

8. 서다   h) to walk

9. 뛰다   i) to run

10. 공부하다   j) to come

✏️ **Writing Practice**

Write the corresponding verb under each picture, copying from the list above.

1. _____ 2. _____ 3. _____ 4. _____

5. _____   6. _____   7. _____

• ADJECTIVES •

Adjectives in Korean function just like verbs; instead of saying "happy," we use the verb form "to be happy." So you can consider the following adjectives as a sort of "descriptive verb."

🎧 GUIDED WRITING PRACTICE

Practice writing each of the following adjectives in the boxes provided.

중요하다　**jungyohada**　to be important

| 중 | 요 | 하 | 다 | | | | | | | | | | | | | |

필요하다　**piryohada**　to be necessary

| 필 | 요 | 하 | 다 | | | | | | | | | | | | | |

아름답다　**areumdapda**　to be beautiful

| 아 | 름 | 답 | 다 | | | | | | | | | | | | | |

맞다　**matda**　to be correct

| 맞 | 다 | | | | | | | | | | | | | | |

재미있다　**jaemiitda**　to be fun

| 재 | 미 | 있 | 다 | | | | | | | | | | | | | |

맛있다　**masitda**　to be delicious

| 맛 | 있 | 다 | | | | | | | | | | | | | |

멋있다　**meositda**　to be cool (fashionable or attractive)

| 멋 | 있 | 다 | | | | | | | | | | | | | |

이상하다　**isanghada**　to be strange

| 이 | 상 | 하 | 다 | | | | | | | | | | | | | |

행복하다　**haengbokhada**　to be happy

| 행 | 복 | 하 | 다 | | | | | | | | | | | | | |

슬프다　**seulpeuda**　to be sad

| 슬 | 프 | 다 | | | | | | | | | | | | | |

예쁘다 **yebbeuda** to be pretty

예	쁘	다										

덥다 **deopda** to be hot

덥	다												

춥다 **chupda** to be cold

춥	다												

좋다 **joda** to be good

좋	다												

나쁘다 **nabbeuda** to be bad

나	쁘	다								

따뜻하다 **ddaddeuthada** to be warm

따	뜻	하	다							

똑똑하다 **ddokddokhada** to be smart

똑	똑	하	다							

피곤하다 **pigonhada** to be tired

피	곤	하	다							

졸리다 **jollida** to be sleepy

졸	리	다								

비싸다 **bissada** to be expensive

비	싸	다								

바쁘다 **babbeuda** to be busy

바	쁘	다								

📖 Reading Practice

Draw lines to match the English word with the Korean word. Practice sounding out the Korean as you go. Check your answers on page 96.

1. 행복하다	a)	to be expensive
2. 맛있다	b)	to be hot
3. 나쁘다	c)	to be correct
4. 비싸다	d)	to be delicious
5. 따뜻하다	e)	to be warm
6. 덥다	f)	to be happy
7. 중요하다	g)	to be sad
8. 맞다	h)	to be sleepy
9. 졸리다	i)	to be important
10. 슬프다	j)	to be bad

✏️ Writing Practice

Write the adjective in Korean that you would use to describe what is listed.

1. The CEO of a company

_____

2. A K-pop idol

_____

3. A summer sunset

_____

4. Korean fried chicken

_____

5. A person at a funeral

_____

6. A winter's day

_____

7. A student in medical school

_____

8. A very nice car

_____

9. The night clerk at a hotel

_____

10. Something else

_____

🎧 **GUIDED WRITING PRACTICE**

Practice writing each of the following words in the boxes provided.

가수 **gasu** singer

가	수											

케이팝 **keipap** K-pop

케	이	팝									

노래 **norae** song

노	래											

춤 **chum** dance

춤													

걸그룹 **geolgeurup** girl group

걸	그	룹							

보이그룹 **boigeurup** boy group

보	이	그	룹							

아이돌 **aidol** idol

아	이	돌							

연예인 **yeonyein** celebrity

연	예	인							

배우 **baeu** actor

배	우											

드라마 **deurama** drama

드	라	마							

영화 **yeonghwa** movie

영	화												

음악 **eumak** music

음	악												

먹방 **meokbang** mukbang

먹	방												

애교 **aegyo** acting cute

애	교												

팬 **paen** fan

팬																

유튜브 **yutyubeu** YouTube

유	튜	브									

📖 Reading Practice

Draw lines to match the English word with the Korean word. Practice sounding out the Korean as you go. Check your answers on page 96.

1. 음악		a)	celebrity
2. 연예인		b)	girl group
3. 보이그룹		c)	music
4. 드라마		d)	drama
5. 아이돌		e)	K-pop
6. 걸그룹		f)	boy group
7. 노래		g)	idol
8. 케이팝		h)	song
9. 배우		i)	movie
10. 영화		j)	actor

🎧 Listening and Reading Practice

Read and listen to the dialogue and underline the words to do with K-pop, dramas or movies. Check your answers on page 96.

주희: 연예인 직접 본 적 있니?
Juhui: Have you ever seen a celebrity in person?

민수: 글쎄. 영화 배우는 본 적 없지만 아이돌은 봤어.
Minsu: Hmm. I've never seen a movie actor but I've seen an idol.

주희: 진짜? 누구 봤는데? 나 케이팝 완전 좋아하거든.
Juhui: Really? Who did you see? I love K-pop.

민수: 이름은 잘 모르겠는데 가수였어.
Minsu: I don't know the name but it was a singer.

주희: 이름 모르면 어떡해? 난 유명한 보이그룹이나 걸그룹 멤버 다 안단 말이야.
Juhui: How could you not know the name? I know the members of all the famous boy groups and girl groups.

민수: 나는 원래 음악 잘 안 듣거든. 드라마나 유튜브 같은 것 많이 보지.
Minsu: I don't really listen to music much. I watch dramas or YouTube videos.

주희: 아 유튜브에서 뭐 봐? 노래 같은 것 많이 찾아서 들어?
Juhui: Ah, what do you watch on YouTube? Do you look up songs to listen to?

민수: 아니. 나는 노래보단 먹방 같은 게 재밌어.
Minsu: No. I think things like mukbangs are more fun than songs.

• SOCIAL MEDIA •

🎧 GUIDED WRITING PRACTICE

Practice writing each of the following social media words in the boxes provided.

페이스북   **peiseubuk**   Facebook

| 페 | 이 | 스 | 북 | | | | | | | | | | | | | |

인스타그램   **inseutageuraem**   Instagram

| 인 | 스 | 타 | 그 | 램 | | | | | | | | | | | |

카카오톡   **kakaotok**   Kakaotalk

| 카 | 카 | 오 | 톡 | | | | | | | | | | | | | |

에스엔에스   **eseueneseu**   SNS

| 에 | 스 | 엔 | 에 | 스 | | | | | | | | | | | |

프로필 사진   **peuropil sajin**   profile picture

| 프 | 로 | 필 | 사 | 진 | | | | | | | | | | | |

친구 추가   **chingu chuga**   add friend

| 친 | 구 | 추 | 가 | | | | | | | | | | | | | |

댓글   **daetgeul**   comment

| 댓 | 글 | | | | | | | | | | | | | | | |

메시지   **mesiji**   message

| 메 | 시 | 지 | | | | | | | | | | | | | |

이모티콘   **imotikon**   emoticon

| 이 | 모 | 티 | 콘 | | | | | | | | | | | | | |

스티커   **seutikeo**   sticker

| 스 | 티 | 커 | | | | | | | | | | | | | |

영상   **yeongsang**   video

영	상											

공유   **gongyu**   share

공	유											

🎧 ✏️ Writing Practice

Look at the English sentence and guess which word is missing. Write the missing word into the Korean sentence. Check your answers by listening to the audio and referring to the answer key on page 96.

1. I have so many friends on _____ that it's hard to keep track of who they all are.

   나 _____ 에 친구가 너무 많아서 다 누구인지 기억하기가 힘들어.

2. Things like photos are posted on _____ more often than text is.

   _____ 에 글보다 사진 같은 것 많이 올리지.

3. Young people these days all make friends while using _____ .

   요즘 젊은 사람들은 다 _____ 쓰면서 친구들 사귀는 것 같아요.

4. There were so many _____ on my new _____ .

   내가 새로 올린 _____ 에 _____ 엄청 많았어.

5. _____ is a great app for sending and receiving _____ .

   _____은 _____ 보낼 때 좋은 애플이다.

6. Older people aren't very good at using _____ or _____ when they send texts.

   나이 드신 분들은 문자 보낼 때 _____ 이나 _____ 같은 것 잘 못 쓰시는 것 같아요.

7. Whenever I see a good _____ I always want to _____ it with my friends.

   나는 좋은 _____ 볼 때마다 항상 친구들이랑 _____ 하고 싶더라.

🎧 **GUIDED WRITING PRACTICE**

Practice writing each of the following words in the boxes provided.

컴퓨터　**keompyuteo**　computer

컴	퓨	터										

인터넷　**inteonet**　Internet

인	터	넷										

와이파이　**waipai**　Wi-Fi

와	이	파	이								

연결　**yeongyeol**　connection

연	결												

노트북　**noteubuk**　laptop

노	트	북										

키보드　**kibodeu**　keyboard

키	보	드										

핸드폰　**haendeupon**　cell phone

핸	드	폰										

스마트폰　**seumateupon**　smartphone

스	마	트	폰								

화면　**hwamyeon**　screen

화	면												

충전기　**chungjeongi**　charger

콘	센	트										

배터리　**baeteori**　battery

배	터	리														

전화　**jeonhwa**　phone

전	화														

통화　**tonghwa**　phone call

통	화														

yeongsangtonghwa　video call

영	상	통	화												

켜다　**kyeoda**　to turn on

켜	다														

끄다　**ggeuda**　to turn off

끄	다														

연결 상태　**yeongyeol sangtae**　connection quality

연	결	상	태												

끊기다　**ggeunhgida**　to break up (a connection)

끊	기	다													

들리다　**deullida**　to be able to hear

들	리	다													

치다　**chida**　to type

치	다														

검색하다　**geomsaekhada**　to search (online)

검	색	하	다												

📖 Reading Practice

Draw lines to match the English word with the Korean word. Practice sounding out the Korean as you go. Check your answers on page 96.

1. 인터넷   a) smartphone

2. 스마트폰   b) cell phone

3. 와이파이   c) charger

4. 충전기   d) keyboard

5. 화면   e) Internet

6. 핸드폰   f) video call

7. 컴퓨터   g) screen

8. 노트북   h) Wi-Fi

9. 영상 통화   i) laptop

10. 키보드   j) computer

🎧 Listening and Reading Practice

Read and listen to the sentences and underline the words to do with phones and computers. Check your answers on page 96.

1. There is almost no one who doesn't have a cell phone these days.
   요즘 핸드폰 없는 사람 거의 없다.

2. If you don't carry your charger with you, you may regret it.
   충전기 안 챙기고 다니면 후회할 수도 있어.

3. Did the screen on your smartphone get cracked?
   스마트폰의 화면이 깨졌어요?

4. If your Wi-Fi connection is not good, you won't be able to use the Internet.
   와이파이 연결이 안 좋으면 인터넷 못 쓸 거예요.

5. Even young students must learn to use computers in today's society.
   어린 학생들도 오늘날의 사회에선 컴퓨터를 쓰는 법을 배워야 해요.

🎧 GUIDED WRITING PRACTICE

Practice writing each of the following words in the boxes provided.

농구   **nonggu**   basketball

농 구								

축구   **chukgu**   soccer

축 구								

테니스   **teniseu**   tennis

테 니 스						

달리기   **dalligi**   running

달 리 기						

복싱   **boksing**   boxing

복 싱								

골프   **golpeu**   golf

골 프								

배드민턴   **baedeuminteon**   badminton

배 드 민 턴					

태권도   **taegwondo**   taekwondo

태 권 도						

요가   **yoga**   yoga

요 가								

사이클링   **saikeulling**   cycling

사 이 클 링					

✏️ Reading and Writing Practice

Label the pictures with words from the box. Check your answers by looking back at page 93.

| 골프 | 복싱 | 달리기 | 축구 | 요가 | 테니스 | 배드민턴 | 태권도 | 농구 | 사이클 |

I. _____ 2. _____ 3. _____

4. _____ 5. _____ 6. _____

7. _____ 8. _____

9. _____ IO. _____

Answer Key

page 13

1. 휴가   ga   hyuga
2. 고양이   go   goyangi
3. 그림   geu   geurim
4. 기분   gi   gibun
5. 거기   geogi   geogi
6. 가구   gagu   gagu

page 15

1. 너무   neo   neomu
2. 느낌   neu   neuggim
3. 노래   no   norae
4. 바나나   nana   banana
5. 누나   nuna   nuna
6. 어머니   ni   eomeoni

page 17

1. 라디오   di   radio
2. 다리   da   dari
3. 포도   do   podo
4. 두부   du   dubu
5. 더위   deo   deowi
6. 드라마   deu   deurama

page 19

1. 도로   ro   doro
2. 하루   ru   haru
3. 달러   reo   dalleo
4. 라면   ra   ramyeon
5. 고르다   reu   goreuda
6. 머리   ri   meori

page 20

1. 모자   mo   moja
2. 무릎   mu   mureup
3. 마음   ma   maeum
4. 할머니   meo   halmeoni
5. 미국   mi   miguk
6. 오므라이스   meu   omeuraiseu

page 23

1. 아버지   beo   abeoji
2. 공부   bu   gongbu
3. 티브이   beu   tibeui
4. 바다   ba   bada
5. 비행기   bi   bihaenggi
6. 바보   babo   babo

page 25

1. 시간   si   sigan
2. 버스   seu   beoseu
3. 서로   seo   seoro
4. 가수   su   gasu
5. 사과   sa   sagwa
6. 주소   so   juso

page 27

1. 유아   a   yua
2. 어제   eo   eoje
3. 오이   oi   oi
4. 으뜸   eu   euddeum
5. 우리   u   uri
6. 오늘   o   oneul

page 28

1. 자주   jaju   jaju
2. 저녁   jeo   jeonyeok
3. 지금   ji   jigeum
4. 조금   jo   jogeum
5. 아주   ju   aju
6. 치즈   jeu   chijeu

page 33

1. 초대   cho   chodae
2. 스포츠   cheu   seupocheu
3. 처음   cheo   cheoeum
4. 고추   chu   gochu
5. 녹차   cha   nokcha
6. 치마   chi   chima

page 34

1. 쿠키   kuki   kuki
2. 카드   ka   kadeu
3. 코끼리   ko   koggiri
4. 아이스크림   keu   aiseukeurim
5. 키스   ki   kiseu
6. 커피   keo   keopi

page 36

1. 사투리   tu   saturi
2. 티켓   ti   tiket
3. 아파트   teu   apateu
4. 컴퓨터   teo   keompyuteo
5. 스타일   ta   seutail
6. 토끼   to   toggi

page 38

1. 프랑스   peu   peurangseu
2. 샴푸   pu   syampu
3. 포크   po   pokeu
4. 피자   pi   pija
5. 캠퍼스   peo   kaempeoseu
6. 양파   pa   yangpa

page 39

1. 후배   hu   hubae
2. 흐름   heu   heureum
3. 하나   ha   hana
4. 히잡   hi   hijap
5. 번호   ho   beonho
6. 허리   heo   heori

page 44

1. 두꺼비   ggeo   duggeobi
2. 끄덕   ggeu   ggeudeok
3. 꼬마   ggo   ggoma
4. 까치   gga   ggachi
5. 도끼   ggi   doggi
6. 뻐꾸기   ggu   bbeoggugi

page 46

1. 이따   dda   idda
2. 으뜸   ddeum   euddeum
3. 허리띠   ddi   heoriddi
4. 또래   ddo   ddorae
5. 뚜껑   ddu   dduggeong
6. 따님   dda   ddanim

page 48

1. 뿌리   bbu   bburi
2. 뻐꾹   gguk   bbeogguk
3. 삐삐   bbi   bbibbi
4. 뽀뽀   bbo   bbobbo
5. 오빠   bba   obba
6. 쁘띠   bbeu   bbeuddi

page 49

1. 싸움   ssa   ssaum
2. 일쑤   ssu   ilssu
3. 쏘가리   sso   ssogari
4. 벌써   sseo   beolsseo
5. 날씨   ssi   nalssi
6. 쓰레기   sseu   sseuregi

page 51

1. 쯔유   jjeu   jjeuyu
2. 공짜   jja   gongjja
3. 쭈글쭈글   jju   jjugeuljjugeul
4. 찌개   jji   jjigae

page 55

1. bya
2. gyeo
3. ryo
4. myu
5. dae
6. yae
7. ne
8. hye
9. kwa
10. poe
11. swae
12. two
13. jwe
14. wi
15. chui
16. mwi
17. bwo
18. gya
19. rwae
20. nyo
21. sae
22. dwe
23. yu
24. jyo

25. hyeo　　26. nyae　　27. kui
28. che　　29. oe　　30. pye

page 62

1.	삶	salm	6.	앉	ant
2.	밟	balp	7.	몫	mok
3.	읽	ilk	8.	핥	halt
4.	붉	bulk	9.	훑	heult
5.	꿇	ggulh	10.	끊	ggeun

page 70

Reading Practice: Chinese Numbers

One (d); Two (g); Three (b); Four (j);
Five (c); Six (h); Seven (a); Eight (i);
Nine (f); Ten (e)

Korean Numbers

One (d); Two (b); Three (e); Four (g);
Five (c); Six (i); Seven (f); Eight (a);
Nine (j); Ten (h)

page 70

Listening and Reading Practice

1. 아이들이 여덟 명 있었어.
2. 이 년이 걸렸어요.
3. 그가 고양이 열 마리를 봤어요.
4. 다섯 시간 걸릴 거야.
5. 사과 여섯 개 주세요.
6. 삼 일 동안 잤어요.
7. 구 페이지에 있어요.
8. 그녀의 집이 사 층에 있어요.
9. 칠 일이 있었어요.
10. 그는 일 번을 봤어요.

page 72

Reading Practice

1. h; 2. d; 3. c; 4. b; 5. i; 6. a; 7. g; 8. f; 9.e

Page 72

Listening and Reading Practice

1. 우리집 정원에 빨간색, 노란색, 그리고 보라색 꽃이 있어요.
2. 그녀는 빨간색 옷을 자주 입었다.
3. 검정색 양복을 입고 왔어요.
4. 미국 사람 중에 눈이 파란색인 사람이 많아요.
5. 보라색 동물은 없을 거야.
6. 우리 아버지가 초록색 자동차를 샀어요.
7. 하얀색 구름이 정말 예뻤어.
8. 내 교복은 회색이에요.
9. 주황색은 행복해 보이는 색깔입니다.
10. 내가 가장 좋아하는 색깔은 노란색이에요.

page 74

Family Tree (top to bottom, left to right)

C, G
A, E, D, B
F, H

Page 77

1. Bibimbap, fried rice, kimbap, spicy rice cakes
2. Two:
   a. 매운 맛 치킨　maeun mat chikin
      spicy fried chicken
   b. 간장 치킨　ganjang chikin
      soy sauce fried chicken
3. Pork belly.
4. 5,000 won.
5. Five.

Page 78

Listening and Reading Practice

미나: 호빈아, 밥 먹으러 갈래?
호빈: 응. 김밥이나 떡볶이 먹자.
미나: 김밥은 싫어. 어제 먹었거든. 고기 어때? 불고기나 삼겹살이 땡기네.
호빈: 고기는 비싸잖아. 그냥 치킨으로 할까?
미나: 너무 좋아. 치킨 먹고 맥주 마시자.
호빈: 좋지.
미나: 후식으로 우리 집에서 과일 먹자. 집에 맛있는 복숭아가 있거든.

page 81

Reading Practice

1. c; 2. f; 3. d; 4. h; 5. b; 6. i; 7. a; 8. e; 9. i; 10. g

page 84

Reading Practice

1. f; 2. d; 3. j; 4. a; 5. e; 6. b; 7. i; 8. c; 9. h; 10. g

page 86

Reading Practice

1. c; 2 a; 3. f; 4. d; 5. g; 6. b; 7. h; 8. e; 9. j; 10 i

page 87

Listening and Reading Practice

주희: 연예인 직접 본 적 있니?
민수: 글쎄. 영화 배우는 본 적 없지만 아이돌은 봤어.

주희: 진짜? 누구 봤는데? 나 케이팝 완전 좋아하거든.
민수: 이름은 잘 모르겠는데 가수였어.
주희: 이름 모르면 어떡해? 난 유명한 보이그룹이나 걸그룹 멤버 다 안단 말이야.
민수: 나는 원래 음악 잘 안 듣거든. 드라마나 유튜브 같은 것 많이 보지.
주희: 아 유튜브에서 뭐 봐? 노래 같은 것 많이 찾아서 들어?
민수: 아니. 나는 노래보단 먹방 같은 게 재밌어.

page 89

Writing Practice

1. 나 페이스북에 친구가 너무 많아서 다 누구인지 기억하기가 힘들어.
2. 인스타그램에 글보다 사진 같은 것 많이 올리지.
3. 요즘 젊은 사람들은 다 에스엔에스 쓰면서 친구들 사귀는 것 같아요.
4. 내가 새로 올린 프로필 사진에 댓글 엄청 많았어.
5. 카카오톡은 메시지 보낼 때 좋은 애플이다.
6. 나이 드신 분들은 문자 보낼 때 이모티콘이나 스티커 같은 것 잘 못 쓰시는 것 같아요.
7. 나는 좋은 영상 볼 때마다 항상 친구들이랑 공유하고 싶더라.

page 92

Reading Practice

1. e; 2. a; 3. h; 4. c; 5. g; 6. b; 7. j; 8. i; 9. f; 10. d

page 92

Listening and Reading Practice

1. 요즘 핸드폰 없는 사람 거의 없다.
2. 충전기 안 챙기고 다니면 후회할 수도 있어.
3. 스마트폰의 화면이 깨졌어요?
4. 와이파이 연결이 안 좋으면 인터넷 못 쓸 거예요.
5. 어린 학생들도 오늘날의 사회에선 컴퓨터를 쓰는 법을 배워야 해요.